95

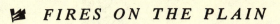 *FIRES ON THE PLAIN*

Translated from the Japa

Fires on the Plain

SHOHEI OOKA

by IVAN MORRIS

GREENWOOD PRESS, PUBLISHERS
WESTPORT, CONNECTICUT

Library of Congress Cataloging in Publication Data

Ōoka, Shōhei, 1909–
    Fires on the plain.

    Translation of Nobi.
    Reprint of the 1st ed. published by Knopf, New York.
    1. World War, 1939-1945--Fiction.   I. Title.
PZ4.O575Fi 1978 [PL835.O5] 895.6'3'5   78-16916
ISBN 0-313-20567-1

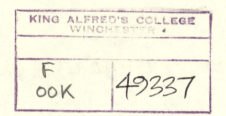
Originally published in Japan as NOBI

Reprinted with the permission of Alfred A. Knopf, Inc.

Reprinted in 1978 by Greenwood Press, Inc.
51 Riverside Avenue, Westport, CT. 06880

Printed in the United States of America

10 9 8 7 6 5 4 3 2 1

CONTENTS

FIRES ON THE PLAIN

1 ❧ DEPARTURE

My squad leader slapped me in the face.

"You damned fool!" he said. "D'you mean to say you let them send you back here? If you'd told them at the hospital you had nowhere to go, they'd have had to take care of you. You know perfectly well there's no room in this company for consumptives like you!"

My eyes were riveted to his lips, which became more and more moist as he babbled away. Why he should be so excited I could not understand, seeing that it was I, not he, who was receiving the fatal sentence. No doubt it was just an instance of the military tendency to raise one's temper automatically as one raised one's voice. I had noticed that as our condition had deteriorated the officers had begun to let loose on us soldiers the nervousness lying beneath their mask of military impassivity. Food was our squad leader's chief preoccupation (as it was indeed of the entire Japanese army in the Philippines) and accordingly the theme of food underlay his present screed.

"Look here, Private Tamura," he continued, "almost all our men are out foraging for food. Don't you under-

stand? We're fighting for our lives! We've no place for
anyone who can't pull his own weight." His voice grew
louder. "You've damned well got to go back to that hospital! If they won't let you in, just plant yourself by the
front door and wait till they do! They'll take care of you
in the end. And if they still refuse, then—well, you'd better put your hand grenade to good use and make an end
to it all. At least you'll be carrying out your final duty to
your country."

I knew perfectly well that however long I "planted"
myself in front of the hospital, I would not be admitted
unless I was equipped with an adequate supply of food.
The Army doctors and medical orderlies depended entirely on the patients for their provisions. The ever-
increasing group of men "planted" outside the hospital
bespoke the futility of seeking admission without this
vital commodity. Like me, these men had all been thrown
out of their companies and left to their fates.

I had suffered a slight hemorrhage shortly after we
landed on the west coast of Leyte in the latter part of No-
vember. While I was stationed in Luzon I had constantly
feared a recurrence of my illness, and this in fact had
come about in the course of our forced march into the
interior of the island following the landing on Leyte.

s promptly given a five-day ration of food and sent
ield hospital in the mountains.

the hospital wounded soldiers were lying about on
h wooden beds that had been requisitioned from
an houses. The men were covered with blood and
but no one seemed to be doing anything for them.
n the doctor saw me, he first lectured me severely
aving come to a field hospital suffering from con-
tion; but when he realized that I had brought my
food, he gave instructions for me to be admitted.
fter I had spent three days in bed, the doctor pro-
ced me cured and I left the hospital. My squad
r, however, did not agree with the doctor's verdict;
rther contended that since I had brought five days'
ns with me, I should have stuck it out in the hospital
he full five days. I was ordered to return. When I re-
ared at the hospital, the doctor indignantly denied
my rations had been sufficient for five days and
d that in any case they had already been used up.

so this morning I had once more found myself
ling back to my unit. I was fully aware that I would
be taken back and was really only curious whether
company would completely abandon one of its men
s fate.

"Yes, sir," I said, my eyes still fixed on the squad leader's humid lips, "I understand perfectly. I am to report back to the hospital. And if I am not admitted, I am to kill myself."

Normally, the squad leader would have objected to the suggestion of individual judgment implied in the words "I understand perfectly," a terse repetition of orders being considered adequate; this time he chose to overlook the peccadillo.

"That's right. And look here, Private Tamura, try to cheer up! Remember—it's all for the Fatherland. To the very end I expect you to act like a true soldier of the Emperor."

"Yes, sir."

In the corner of the room, by the window, the quartermaster sergeant was busy filling out some document. He was sitting with his back turned, in front of the old wooden crate that served as desk. I did not think he was listening, but when I had repeated my orders he got to his feet, and screwing up his eyes so that they became even narrower than usual, said: "That's right, Tamura. I'm sorry we seem to be throwing you out like this, but you must try and look at it from the squad leader's point of view as well. Now don't go and kill yourself unless you absolutely have to," the sergeant added, as if by an afterthought. "Here, I'm going to give you some provisions."

He went to the opposite corner and from a pile of potatoes picked up a few at random in both hands. They were the small Philippine potatoes known as *kamote,* which taste rather like our own sweet potatoes. I thanked him politely, but as I put the potatoes into my haversack my hands were trembling. Six small potatoes—to this extent and no further was my country prepared to guarantee my survival: this country of mine to which I was offering my life. There was a terrifying mathematical exactness about this number six.

I saluted, made a rightabout-face, and opened the door. As I left the room the squad leader's voice followed me into the passage. "Don't bother to report to the company commander!" he shouted.

In the back of my mind had lurked a hope—a hope that if I spoke to the company commander he might possibly intercede on my behalf. I suppose that even at this stage I vaguely thought that I might contrive to remain with my unit. At the other end of the short passage I could see the company commander's room. A straw mat hanging over the entrance gave it an air of utter calm. But now the squad leader's last words had expunged my final hope. Obviously the company commander had

already settled my case when he sent me back to the
pital the day before. My return this afternoon ha
effect changed nothing: all that had remained wa
the squad leader to pronounce sentence.

As I descended the half-rotted stairs I noticed
the sun shone down through the cracks in the wood,
ing neat patterns on the ground below. In front o
building stood rows of bushes, interspersed with f
tropical plants; beyond these was a clump of trees w
a group of soldiers busied themselves digging an
aircraft trench. They were using sticks and old
(requisitioned from civilian houses) by way of sho
Our company had in fact become no more than a br
group of stragglers skulking in a small mountain
lage; for some time the Americans had no longer
bothered to bomb us. Yet the antiaircraft trench s
how gave us a sense of security, and, besides, there
no other work to be done at the camp.

In the shade of the trees, the soldiers' faces were
and expressionless; one of the men looked up in
direction but immediately turned aside and conti
his digging. Most of these soldiers were conscripts
had come here from Japan at the same time as m
The boredom of life on the troopship had brought u
gether and given us a certain sense of kinship; but v

we arrived in the Philippines and were assigned to units with veteran troops, we soon began to sink back into our normal egotism. Then we landed on Leyte Island and our real difficulties began.

Before long any comradeship that we had once felt for each other had virtually disappeared. When I felt ill and was on the way to becoming a burden to the other men, I noticed a growing chill in their attitude toward me. For people like us, living day and night on the brink of danger, the normal instinct of survival seems to strike inward, like a disease, distorting the personality and removing all motives other than those of sheer self-interest. That is why this afternoon I did not wait to go and tell my former comrades-in-arms what had happened to me. For one thing, they probably already knew; besides, it seemed unfair to risk awakening their dormant sense of humanity.

Beside a roadside tree was gathered a group of sentries—all that remained of our company's effective military strength. We had landed on the west coast of Leyte as part of a mixed brigade, which in turn belonged to one of several Army corps that had been sent to relieve the desperate position of the Japanese forces in the Tacloban area. At the beach we had been met by a massive American air attack; half of our men had been killed, and all heavy equipment sunk together with the transports. The surviving half of our corps was then ordered to proceed eastward, according to plan, along the narrow path that crossed the island's central mountain range. Our objective was Burauen airfield, but we had only just reached the foot of the mountains when we ran into the scattered remnants of another Army corps, which had set out ahead of us. It appeared that they had been turned back by an American flying column armed with trench mortars.

We now tried to cross the mountains farther south where there was no path at all, but as soon as we started to climb we were subjected to a fierce trench-mortar attack from three directions. We returned at the double to the foot of the mountains and deployed. The various companies spread out over the valley and pitched camp; a liaison officer was dispatched to the base at Ormoc for further instructions. When he returned, the rumor spread among the soldiers that headquarters had sent us orders to force our way across the mountains, but that our C.O. had torn them up in disgust.

Be that as it may, our company, which by now had been decimated to the size of a platoon, remained in a small village in the valley. The rations, brought with us from Ormoc, were soon exhausted, nor was it long before we had finished the corn and other cereals that the Filipino inhabitants had left behind when they abandoned their houses. Our activities became concentrated on searching for potatoes, bananas, and any other food that we could lay our hands on in the near-by fields and hills.

For the purpose of these foraging expeditions our company was divided into three groups. One group would go and live off the land for a few days; when they returned, they would bring enough food for themselves and for the third group to live on while the second group went out in its turn. Often on these expeditions they would run into members from other units and fierce arguments would ensue as to which company had the preferential rights in such and such an area. Inevitably the distance and duration of the foraging trips became longer as the weeks went by.

After my hemorrhage I was not fit to carry heavy loads and therefore could not take part in the foraging. From this stemmed the ineluctable order to go and kill myself.

As I made my way between the trees toward the sentries they looked up at me in silent greeting. I dreaded having to repeat my formal report to the N.C.O. in charge; even more, I hated exposing myself to their apathetic sympathy. I felt that they were all waiting for

the fateful words, "I've been thrown out," and it seem
ages before I reached the tree trunk around which th
were gathered.

The lance corporal's pale face was impassive while
listened to my report. Yet when I had finished, I co
see that he was moved, as if my fate had reminded h
of his own uneasiness about the future.

"I really don't know who's better off," he mutter
"you or we. It won't be long now before they'll be ord
ing us to mass for a final breakthrough. At least you'll
getting out of that!"

"I don't suppose they'll let you into the hospi
though," said one of the soldiers.

I smiled.

"If they don't let me in, I've just got to wait till t
do," I said, repeating the squad leader's words. But
this time I was wondering how to bring the scene to
end as quickly as possible.

When I said good-by, I noticed that one of the sold
with whom I exchanged glances had a twisted look on
face. I wondered if the twisted look that I felt on my
face was catching, like a yawn.

Thus I left my company.

⚑
⚑

⚑ 2 ⚑ *THE FOREST PATH*

In the center of the village towered a huge acacia tree, casting its shadow over its own roots, which stretched across the dusty road. The empty houses were closed and shuttered; the village was utterly deserted. The brown, shining volcanic gravel spread out from the village over the green, sun-drenched fields.

I felt a crushing sense of despair; yet at the same time I was aware of a certain dormant happiness stirring within me. For at last I was free. To be sure, my freedom lay simply in the fact that no one cared any longer where I went or what I did. But at least I was free to spend these last days of my life, not as a soldier under orders, but as I myself wished.

I had already decided on my destination: I was going back to the hospital. This was not out of any vain hope of being admitted as a patient. No, I simply wanted to meet the men who were "planted" there in front of the building. Nor did I have any special aim in this; I was only interested in *looking* once more at these people who, like me, had nowhere to go.

When I left the village, I could see the fields spread out

in all directions. About half a mile straight ahead to the north they were bounded by a forest. On the right, the flat paddy fields stretched into the distance as far as the volcanic mountain range that formed the spine of Leyte Island. One low branch of the mountains extended to the left and formed a backdrop to the forest ahead of me; it was curved gently like the smooth back of a recumbent woman. Far to the left its undulations came to an end with a small hummock, and at this point I could make out a rapid river about twenty yards wide. The mountains rose steeply again on the opposite bank and followed the river downstream. Beyond these mountains must have lain the ocean. The hospital was about four miles straight ahead, through the forest and over the hills.

The afternoon sun was dazzling, and yet the clear, shining sky was pregnant with storm. An enemy plane flew round and round in the same spot, the insect buzz of its engines interrupted now and then by the staccato sound of our antiaircraft guns firing sporadically from somewhere in the mountains. Walking here through the open fields, I risked being strafed by the plane, but in my present predicament this danger failed to worry me.

My handkerchief under my cap to catch the perspiration and my rifle in my shoulder-strap, I strode along at a sprightly pace. I had a temperature, I realized, but fever had by now become part of my normal existence. If I was to live this final period in my own free way, I must disregard such things as temperatures: and illness, when all hope of a cure has gone, is no such great matter.

Walking along, I occasionally had to stop by the side of the road to spit out the mucus that kept rising in my throat. It rather pleased me to think of the malignant tubercle bacilli that I had brought from Japan being scorched to death under the tropical sun.

At the entrance to the forest the road divided into two. Straight ahead was the path that crossed the hills and led directly to the opposite valley where lay the hospital. The left-hand fork circled the hummock by the river and eventually emerged into the same valley. The path over the hills was, of course, far shorter, but having already taken it three times in the past twenty-four hours, I decided on the spur of the moment to try the unfamiliar circuitous route.

It was dark within the forest. On either side of the narrow path towered huge oaklike trees; the space between them was densely filled with unfamiliar brushwood and shrubs that stretched out the tentacles of their vines and creepers in all directions. The ground was thick with moldering leaves, which here in the tropics kept falling regardless of the season; the surface of the

path felt soft as rubber under my feet. The newly fallen
leaves made a rustling sound that reminded me of the
road through Musashi Plain at home. With my head
bowed I walked along.

A thought struck me then with great force: *I was
walking along this path for the first time in my life, and
yet I would never walk along it again.* I stopped and
looked about. A deathlike hush hovered over the enormous trees. With their straight trunks, their widely
spread branches, and their broad leaves, they looked
much like our oak trees in Japan; only their names I did
not know. Here they had stood for decades and decades
before I passed beneath them, and here they would continue to stand long after my death. To be sure, there was
nothing strange in this thought, nor in the thought that
I would never again walk through this unknown Philippine forest. What was strange was the complete con-
tradiction existing in my mind between the knowledge
that I was passing here for the first time and the certainty
that I would never pass here in the future.

This was by no means the first time since leaving
Japan that I had been struck by such irrational ideas.
For example, in June, when our troopship was passing
through the Pacific and I stood on deck vaguely gazing

to sea, I had suddenly seen myself impersonally, as
sometimes does in dreams, as part of a tidy, well-
ered scene. The dark-blue, monochrome sea stretched
in all directions to form a perfect circle girded by the
izon; the waters seemed to be forced up all round
circumference, so that we, who were in the center,
upied a sort of hollow. Not far from the water's sur-
hovered a flat-bottomed cloud, formed like the
-tiered rice cakes offered at Shinto shrines; as the
glided smoothly along, the cloud kept its exact shape
remained at the same position astern, rotating slowly
a fan. With the regular sound of the waves lapping
sides of the ship and the monotonous hum of the die-
engines, the whole orderly scene suddenly struck me
ery *strange*.

felt a peculiar excitement—an excitement tinged
somehow pleasurable pain. Perhaps it derived from
fact that at that moment I had an unconscious presen-
ent of my defeat and death. Normally, had I stood
e on deck observing the odd cloud and the accom-
ying dreamlike scene, I would in the back of my
d have imagined myself describing it all some weeks
r to my friends at home who had not had the good
une to sail across the Pacific. Did not my excitement

and pain arise precisely from my knowledge that I would never have the chance of returning home to describe my experiences?

Again, was it not this same presentiment of death that made it seem so strange to me now that I should never again walk along this path in the Philippine forest? In our own country, even in the most distant or inaccessible part, this feeling of strangeness never comes to us, because subconsciously we know that there is always a possibility of our returning there in the future. Does not our entire life-feeling depend upon this inherent assumption that we can *repeat indefinitely* what we are doing at the moment?

I felt not the slightest sorrow at the knowledge of my approaching death. Perhaps it was this very foreknowledge that recently had so enhanced the joy I experienced in nature—in the tropical nature of these Philippine Islands. The soft sensation under my boots when I had walked across the lawn in front of Manila Castle, the dazzling vermilion of the bougainvillæa washed by a sudden squall, the bright red and yellow of the sky at dawn and sunset, the purple-tinted volcanoes, the coral reefs encircling the foaming white waves, the shadowy woods by the ocean's edge—all this had begun to fill my heart with a joy verging on ecstasy. I thanked fate which thus before my death had deigned to show me the beauty and abundance of life. My existence hitherto had been less rich than I might have wished; but it seemed that now at the end I was being blessed by fate—by fate, or, had I not so resolutely refused the word, by God.

Fundamentally, I suppose, my recent confusion of thought and feeling derived from the fact that the equilibrium between my inner consciousness and the outer world had begun to break down. This process had started when I was being transported across the ocean to fight and kill, and I suddenly had realized that I had not the slightest will either to fight or to kill.

My growing fascination with the natural beauty of the Philippines was itself a symptom of my abnormal state of mind. A successful infantryman must look at nature only from the standpoint of necessity. A gentle hollow in the ground is nothing but a shelter from artillery fire, the beautiful green fields simply dangerous terrain that must be crossed at the double. Indeed to the foot soldier, as he is shoved around from place to place, depending on the particular tactics of the day, nature in all her sundry aspects is essentially meaningless. It is this very lack of meaning that supports his existence and provides the wellspring of his courage. Now if, as a result of cowardice or of introspection, this solid carapace of meaninglessness should crack, what is revealed beneath is something even more meaningless for living men: it is, in fine, a presentiment of death.

❦
❦
❦ 3 ❦ *FIRES ON THE PLAIN*

Without knowing it, I had begun to walk once more along the forest path. It ran parallel to the low branch of the mountain, which undulated gently within the forest, and as I walked I could see the green of the hills gleaming through the trees on my right. Now and then, when the forest thinned, the undergrowth that provided this fantastic green cloak spread down as far as the roadside. A row of stunted trees traced the line of the hilltop; standing there by themselves, they looked like a column of men.

The forest came to an end, emerging into a large plain where tufts of grass grew sparsely among the sand and gravel. This was a dry river bed. Scattered here and there like islands, clusters of tall rushes glistened silver-bright in the late afternoon sun. In the center of the scene that stretched out before me, the river formed a single steel

ιd gliding rapidly along the far edge of the plain.
ιss the river rose a hill as high as Mount Yoko in
a County at home. The green covering of the hill
ιed with the light green of the grass by the river
ι. The great hill sloped smoothly upstream, but a
before it reached ground level it dropped off sharply
ιcome a steep cliff. From the dry river bed at the
ιm of the cliff rose a single pillar of black smoke.
came, no doubt, from one of the bonfires one saw
ten in the Philippines at this time of the year. Since
ιad landed in the islands fires like this, in which the
inos burned the husks of their corn after harvest,
ιed to have been almost constantly on our horizon.
ι were, in fact, our only evidence of the continued
ιnce of the native inhabitants, who surrounded us
ιl sides but whom we hardly ever saw. One of the
duties of the sentries was to detect these fires and
ιdge from the shape of the smoke whether they were
ιne bonfires for burning waste husks, or signal fires
ι guerrillas as a primitive means of communicating
ιmation to their distant comrades.
ιe column of smoke that now rose across the river
ιarge and vigorous: it almost certainly came from a
bonfire. Besides, the fire was in an open plain,
ιeas the sinister smoke signals were almost always

lit in more inaccessible places. Yet, coming upon it like this by myself, I felt a shock of fear. Even admitting that it was a genuine bonfire, there must be some person standing over there beside it . . . and this person must be a Filipino . . . and for us all Filipinos were enemies.

For the first time, I regretted having chosen this unfamiliar route; but, now that I had embarked on my journey, whose final destination could in any case only be death, it seemed odious to turn back. I studied the terrain in the direction of the hospital, my glance following the path as it crossed the huge plain and finally disappeared into a forest straight ahead. Directly on my right lay another forest where there seemed to be no path at all, and I decided to avoid the exposed river bed and to make a detour through this forest; later I would join the path at the far end of the plain.

I had to use my bayonet to cut away the ivy that coiled around my legs and to hack at the low branches that blocked my path. Several times my unwieldy Army boots slipped on the swampy, leaf-covered ground. So as not to lose my way, I kept my eyes constantly on the edge of the forest, where the bright reflection of light from the plain lit the ferns in emerald. Suddenly I came upon a path leading to the interior of the forest. I followed it a short distance till it reached a clearing where there was a hut. Next to the hut stood a Filipino. He was looking at me with wide-open eyes. I stopped, leveled my rifle, and quickly glanced round.

"Good day, sir," said the Filipino, in a cringing tone. He was an unhealthy-looking man of about thirty. From his faded blue breeches emerged a pair of dirty, emaciated legs. I wondered what he could be doing in this area where few, if any, of the native inhabitants remained.

"Hello," I answered mechanically in my bad Visayan, and once more I examined the surroundings. It was completely quiet and the air was redolent with a peculiar smell. Through the open door I could see the interior of the hut, which was raised off the ground by stilts.

"You are welcome, sir," said the man, laughing nervously, his eyes fixed on my rifle.

To my surprise, I heard myself ask: "Have you any corn?"

The man's face clouded over slightly, but he repeated: "You are welcome, sir," as he walked round to the back of the hut. I followed him. A large iron pot hung over a fire and in it bubbled a mushy yellow liquid. Next to the pot was a heap of yellow mountain potatoes; I realized that the unpleasant smell came from these potatoes, which were being boiled down for their juice.

In a separate pot ears of corn were cooking. The
scooped a helping of corn onto a dirty wax dish, a
some coarse-grained black salt and handed it to me.
mediately I knew that I had not the slightest app

"Is this your own house?" I asked.

"No," he said, "I live over there—on the other si
the river."

He pointed through the trees in the direction
which I had come. I did not see why he should
walked all this way to do his cooking. Perhaps this
one of the few places where one could still find pota

"What's that juice for?" I asked, pointing to the
pot; but I could not understand his answer.

I sat on the ground with the dish in front of me.
man was still staring at me with a forced smile.

"Aren't you going to eat, sir?" he asked.

I shook my head and at the same time emptie
corn that he had given me into my haversack. I fel
gusted at myself for taking his food when I was not
gry.

Already I had begun to relax my guard. The
seemed harmless enough. To be sure, we Japanese
diers had had little opportunity or inclination to
about the Filipinos, but, so far as I could judge, the
thing in this fellow's mind, as he squatted there lo

straight at me with his fixed smile, was the simple desire of the conquered subject to curry favor with the tyrant.

All of a sudden, as if he had hit on a brilliant idea, he said: "Wouldn't you like some potatoes?"

"The ones next to the pot?"

"No, no. I've got some much better ones. Just wait here a minute, sir. I'll go and fetch them for you."

He jumped to his feet and hurried into the forest. I followed him vacantly with my eyes as he ran straight along the path without turning around and finally disappeared down a slope.

I examined the interior of the hut. The floorboards were filthy and cracked, the bamboo props were bent, and on the rough board walls crawled a lizard. I realized that it was in such bare and dilapidated hovels that most Filipino peasants spent their lives, without hope of ever acquiring anything beyond the barest essentials. Suddenly it occurred to me that by joining myself to these people, I might somehow find a means of survival. . . .

Some time passed and still the man did not return with the potatoes. I recalled his agile movements as he had stood up and began to feel uneasy. I hurried down the path to the point where he had disappeared. I looked about. The huge trees stood there silently. "He's given me the slip!" I thought, and was overcome by anger. I ran to the edge of the forest and, sure enough, there he was, dashing at full speed across the plain toward the river.

As he neared the bank he stopped for a moment and turned round. Recognizing me, he shook his fist threateningly above his head. I could not possibly shoot him at this distance. He continued running and before long his body was hidden in the glittering rushes.

I smiled grimly. Having seen the impotent hatred in the eyes of the Filipinos in Manila, I should have realized the futility of seeking their friendship. I walked back to the hovel, kicked over the pot of steaming potatoes, and left. This now had become a dangerous place to stay.

From the fact that the man had fled across the river, I gathered that his companions were all on the other side. Accordingly I no longer hesitated to show myself in the open plain. Hurrying over the dry gravel, I approached the point where the path entered the forest ahead; I was determined to be out of the way when that man returned with his companions.

In the forest the trees were small, with narrow trunks. There were anthills on both sides of the path, and ants were gushing forth in a constant stream. I advanced cautiously. My encounter with the Filipino had robbed me of all sense of security, and I was no longer in the mood for abstract meditation.

When the trees began to thin out, I looked back. I could still see the smoke across the river, but now there were two fires rising from the base of the cliff. And from the summit of the hill, which from here looked like a man crouching with his back turned, rose a third column of smoke.

The smoke at the foot of the hill poured straight upward, quickly and vigorously, in two thick pillars; but the smoke at the summit was thin and elegant and, after rising to a certain height, broke off in the high-blowing wind, becoming wispy like the end of a broom; and far up in the sky it shook and fluttered, as though frolicking with the breeze. It was strange to see these two completely different types of fire so close to each other. From my experience standing guard I felt sure that the fire on the hilltop came from burning grass and was in fact a smoke signal.

The path now began to describe a great arc, following the foot of the mountain that separated the hospital from the camp. The contour of the mountain, which from the south had resembled the graceful line of a woman's back, was from this side strangely narrow and forbidding.

From the summit two narrow ridges sloped down like a pair of straddling legs, and in a hollow of one of the ridges I noticed a greenish-brown rock formation shaped exactly like an armchair. The valley for which I was heading should lie just beyond the first ridge. I quickened my pace.

The path entered still another forest and again divided into two, one branch running more or less parallel with the course of the river and the other following the line of the central mountain range. I took the second path and soon emerged onto an enormous grassy plain. And here I saw yet another prairie fire.

The forest stretched to my left in the direction of the sea and disappeared in the distance. Ahead of me the plain rose and fell like a huge sand dune until half a mile away it reached a bare rock formation, which blocked my view like a screen. Halfway between me and the rock the grass was burning across the plain in a strip some sixty yards wide. There was no one in sight.

I stopped in my tracks and gazed at the smoke. Surely it could not be because of *me* that these fires were being lit on the plains. The chance of killing a single Japanese soldier could hardly warrant the effort of starting all these smoke signals. It must be simply a coincidence that

I had chosen a route along which the Filipinos happened to be lighting their prairie fires.

I was seized by a terrible uneasiness, though this did not derive from fear that the guerrillas were conspiring my death. Rather, it belonged to the same strange confusion of feelings which had plagued me intermittently since I had left Japan aboard the troopship. To be sure, I realized that these fires on the plains meant that enemies were lurking near by, but the terror inspired by the columns of smoke came not from this, but from the *order* of the recent events and from the *number* of the fires. It was no doubt my sense of utter isolation from the rest of humanity that made these irrational fancies so much more frightening than any logical fears.

I tried to dispel the growing atmosphere of sorcery by studying my bearings. From the width of the plain I gathered that it must be part of the valley for which I was aiming; and, sure enough, there in the far right-hand corner, by the foot of the rocks, I could make out a cluster of familiar buildings. I set off briskly. Now at least I would have companions—people to whom I could talk. I had no other thought in mind.

Since the path crossed directly through the burning belt of grass, I branched off to the right through the shoulder-high rushes. Yet, as I headed toward the houses I could not take my eyes off the prairie fires. The sun was sinking rapidly and a wind had sprung up. The smoke crawled along the grass, covering it like a white cloak; now and then it would rise suddenly in wool-like tufts and blow away in the direction of the forest that stretched toward the sea.

I could not see a soul on the entire plain. Where were the people who had lit these fires? There was no one and nothing to tell me.

🦋
🦋
🦋 4 🦋 *THE REJECTS*

I approached the hospital compound, passing through the fields where the villagers had cut the grass and planted corn. The bare ridges between the harvested fields reached all the way to the foothills ahead of me. I looked up at the mountain, which again displayed the same voluptuous curves as when I had left camp early that afternoon. But, now that I was close to it, I could see that the beautiful green covering was merely a tangle of rough brushwood which straggled unevenly to the summit, interspersed with patches of ugly red clay.

The compound consisted of three wooden buildings that had formerly been civilian houses. One was used as an office and the other two as wards. Here two Army doctors and seven orderlies looked after about fifty patients. Everything was in short supply. Bandages were never changed and no medicine was provided. Originally the hospital had been on the coast, but in the course of military operations it had been moved inland, together with the thirty-odd patients who had been fit to walk. These constituted the nucleus of the present inmates; no other soldiers were admitted unless they brought sufficient rations.

The only concern of the doctors was how to get rid of their patients and save food. If any man showed even the slightest symptoms of diarrhea, his rations were immediately stopped. In such cases, the patient often preferred to leave the hospital, however ill he might be, rather than to starve slowly to death. On his departure, he would receive one day's supply of food, to live on while he searched for his original unit.

Some of these men were able to walk only a few hundred yards from the hospital before they collapsed by the side of the path. For a few days they would crawl about from place to place, and occasionally one would come upon them at some distance from the hospital, lying under a tree or by the edge of the forest; then they disappeared. Others, who could not move or who did not want to move, "planted" themselves by the side of the forest some twenty yards from the hospital. Their numbers were gradually increasing.

I was exhausted now as I made my way over the hard stubble of the corn to where these soldiers were "planted." Finally I sat down and drank some water from my canteen. I was overcome by a numb feeling of desolation, the result partly of physical exhaustion and partly of the loneliness of the huge plain across which I had come. It was ages now since I had first seen the familiar hospital buildings in the distance, yet it had seemed that I would never reach them. Clustered there compactly beyond the billowing sea of rushes, they had looked so close that I had almost felt I could reach out and touch them. I was awed by the immensity of this plain, which surrounded me on all sides and which had kept me so long from my destination. All the time, the wind soughed gently past my ears on its way across the wide empty fields. The tall rushes bowed their heads in unison, as if being trampled by some invisible giant's foot, and remained prostrate and motionless. . . .

I heard a voice behind me. "What, are you here again?"

I turned around and saw the expressionless face of a middle-aged soldier called Yasuda whom I had met that morning on my way from the hospital. He was suffering from tropical ulcers and one of his legs had swollen to the size of a huge club. On the shin was an ulcer as large as a biscuit, in the center of which the bone was exposed like a grain of boiled rice. Yasuda had adopted the local remedy of wrapping the leaf of an aromatic plant round his leg, applying a small piece of tin over the leaf, and securing it all with a piece of cotton.

"That's right. They wouldn't take me back in my company. They sent me back here again."

"It won't do you much good coming here, you know," said Yasuda.

I wanted to say that I had come, not to be admitted to the hospital, but simply in the hope of joining the squatters. The words stuck in my throat as I realized that what had originally been an *interest* had, during my solitary walk through the forests and plains, become a *necessity*. I could not tell him how desperate I was to belong once more to a group of living people.

"I had nowhere else to go," I said vaguely.

I looked round and counted my companions-in-despair who were sitting here by the edge of the forest. We were eight soldiers in all; of the six who had been here when I had passed in the morning, one had left, and there had been two new arrivals apart from myself.

Only one of us was completely immobile. He was a young soldier who had been thrown out of the hospital a few days before in the last stages of malaria for having annoyed one of the orderlies. The others were suffering from diarrhea, beriberi, tropical ulcers, bullet wounds— or a combination of these complaints; they could have left at any time, had they known of a worth-while destination.

Like me, they were the rejects, the debris of a defeated army. At this stage of the campaign, they could be of no possible military use. Once these men had been discarded from their own units, why should the hospitals bother to take care of them? Yet somehow the field hospital remained, in their imagination, from the days when they had still been on active duty, as the soldier's final haven, his last resort; and so they hovered near the compound, knowing full well that they could die in agony before they would ever be admitted.

I had often observed them during my stay in the hospital as an official patient. No doubt I already at that time had a presentiment that before long I would be joining their numbers. From the ward they had looked like a large stain spread over the forest's edge; they had lain about in all directions without rhyme or reason. Occasionally one of them would get up and move around sluggishly for no particular purpose. They had seemed more like animals than human beings; they resembled, in fact, domestic animals who have been turned out of their homes and who wander about helplessly, uprooted and perplexed.

Now that I was one of them, however, I found to my surprise that there was a certain self-contained calm about these men. It was clear from their expressions that each was guarding his own private personality, that each had his individual needs and moreover a spirit which still strove to tackle these needs. Even their movements, which from the ward had seemed so pointless, now began to acquire a meaning.

Shortly after I arrived, for instance, one of the men, who had been dozing a few yards away, stood up and came over to me.

"How much food have you got?" he asked.

He was fearfully emaciated and I could tell that he was suffering from diarrhea; for, even as he awaited my answer, his whole body shook uncontrollably.

"Six potatoes," I said.

The man nodded with an air of satisfaction and tottered back to his place. Evidently he felt it necessary to know exactly how much food each person had.

"Ha, ha! Six spuds! You're a real millionaire, aren't you?" said a young soldier who was lying near me. He was one of the new arrivals. On his ankle was a bullet wound infested with maggots.

"I wish I'd been in your unit," he continued. "In my company they only give us two spuds when we're thrown out. And now I've just got one left."

He carefully produced the potato from his pocket and held it up for everyone to see. From the silence that immediately fell all around, it was clear that to call attention to the scantiness of one's resources was a breach of local etiquette. The young man took in the situation.

"Don't worry," he said with a sarcastic grunt. "I'm not asking any of you bastards to help me! I can manage for myself. I'm going over there tonight to see what I can pinch."

He glared in the direction of the hospital office.

"Oh, what's going to happen to us?" said a voice, rather in the melodramatic tone of an actor in a radio play. It came from a young man who had belonged to the same company as Yasuda, the middle-aged soldier who had first spoken to me on my arrival. His face was swollen with undernourishment and beriberi and looked enormous over his sunken chest.

"Happen to us!" said the one-potato soldier with a sneer. "We'll die—that's what's going to happen to us! But it's not only us. Everyone who's on this damned island is finished! Anyhow, it's no good worrying about it now."

"What about the parachute unit they said we could expect? It should be here any day now," said another soldier.

"Pshaw! Have you seen a single one of our planes since we landed on this island? They don't dare to show themselves in daylight. They just flap around at night like a lot of damned bats! And the last few nights they haven't even done that. If any parachute units are landing, it'll be the Americans. Except that they aren't going to mess about with parachutes. They'll be landing in LST's—right over there."

He pointed toward the west coast.

"It won't be all that easy for them, you know," said another soldier, joining the conversation. "After all, we still control the west."

"I wouldn't be so sure about that," said the one-potato soldier. "Hear that firing? That's the Americans shelling Ormoc. They'll be here before we know it. Listen!"

The distant thunder of shellfire reverberated in the sky to our north. It was a harsh roar, completely different from the familiar dry sound of trench mortars. As it boomed southward across the plain, striking the mountains behind us and echoing from valley to valley, we could feel the earth trembling.

"It's a twenty-five caliber," said one of the soldiers.

We were all silent, listening intently to the artillery fire.

"Well, what the hell's the difference?" said the one-potato soldier, in his usual sneering tone. "It mightn't be such a bad thing if the Americans did come. After all, now that we've been kicked out of our units, I don't see why we should try to behave like a bunch of damned heroes! We might as well all be taken prisoner and have done with it!"

"They'd kill us, though," said another soldier, who was squatting at some distance from us.

"Kill us? Why the hell should they kill us? Those fellows even believe it's an honor to be a P.O.W. As soon as an American is taken prisoner, everyone automatically thinks he's put up a terrific fight until the moment he was captured. They think the world of prisoners. They'll give us so much corned beef to eat we won't know what to do with it!"

"Shut up!" said the young malarial soldier, rising unsteadily to his feet. His cheeks were flushed and his eyes bloodshot. "You dare to talk like that and still call yourself Japanese!"

The one-potato soldier looked steadily ahead, with a fixed sneer, while the malarial soldier grew more and more excited. I thought he was going to speak again, but instead he just cleared his throat and collapsed on the ground.

📖
📖
📖 5 📖 *PURPLE SHADOWS*

The day was finally drawing to an end. The sky was red with the afterglow of sunset and the peaks of the central mountain range were brightly tinted. On the ground it was growing dark; even the spaces between the blades of grass were filled with purple shadows. The sweet-sour smell of the tropical night rose from the earth. Far away over the hills across the river was a line of twisted clouds, standing next to each other like a row of caterpillars; they, too, were tinted bright red. The prairie fires had died down and nothing remained of them but wisps of smoke rising all around like steam. The wind had fallen.

In the hospital wards, about twenty yards from where we lay, it was evidently supper time. The orderlies were hurrying to and fro with mess trays. One of the doctors—a man about forty, who did not look like a regular Army officer—stood in front of the office and gazed at the glowing sky. He gave a deep sigh and for an instant glanced in our direction. Then he hurried back to the building.

There was a lively hum from the compound, but here by the edge of the forest it was quiet.

"Well, it's about time for us to have a bite, too," said Yasuda. He stood up and walked to where the malarial soldier was lying. "Look here, pal," he said, "if you've still got a spud left, I'll go and boil it for you with my own."

The soldier half opened his eyes, shook his head, and rolled over on his other side. I wondered whether it was that he did not want to eat, or that he had no food left.

Leaning on the branch that he used as a cane, Yasuda hobbled into the interior of the forest. His retreating figure seemed to say: "The rest of you can go and boil your own damned potatoes!"

The one-potato soldier followed Yasuda with eyes full of hatred.

"The filthy swine!" he said. "Cooking spuds for himself in these conditions! He knows how to take care of himself, all right. He's got a whole lot of tobacco leaves hidden away somewhere in the forest. And he's got great wads of the stuff wrapped round his belly. He's just been over to the hospital to trade some of it for spuds. The bastard! He could go back to his unit this minute if he wanted to. Instead he stays here and does a roaring business."

"What's it matter to you?" said the young soldier from Yasuda's company. "Are you jealous or something?"

"Pshaw!" said the one-potato soldier. "You make me sick—the way you always stick up for that old bastard! Does he slip you a slice of potato every now and then so that you'll take his side?"

There was no answer.

The soldiers began to take out their food and eat. Usually their meals consisted of pieces of raw potato; some of the men, however, spread out bits of crumpled paper—rice-ball wrappings that they had managed to save—and carefully picked off the grains of rice and stuck them into their mouths.

The daily hospital ration of one rice ball was served every evening at sundown, and for some reason our own scanty meals by the edge of the forest conformed rigorously to this schedule.

I opened my haversack and munched some of the corn I had taken from the Filipino. Then I took out another handful and gave it to the soldier who had only one potato. He raised his eyebrows in amazement.

"Thank you, thank you very much," he stammered. "But don't worry, I'll pay you back tomorrow." He picked the grains up one by one and popped them into his mouth.

The young soldier who had been arguing with him a few minutes before sidled up to us. His eyes were shining.

"Scram!" said the one-potato soldier, pushing him away. Now and then he glanced at me hopefully; but my largesse was exhausted. Finally he let out a groan and walked off. At that moment I looked straight at him and saw what a tremendous effort he was making at self-control. I realized that he had absolutely no food left. Clearly I had made a mistake in choosing the order of my generosity. But it was too late; in any case, I told myself, if I had not taken the corn in the first place, no one would have had anything from me.

The one-potato soldier had now finished eating.

"Thank you," he said to me. "I shall never forget your kindness—not as long as I live."

"At this rate, I'm afraid it won't be all that long," I said, laughing, "not for any of us."

"That's right," he said. "But at least tonight I'm going to stock up for a few more days. As soon as it's really dark, I'm going to slip into the hospital and pinch any food I can lay my hands on."

"I wouldn't if I were you," I said. I was about to add that he would merely be taking food away from the other patients, but such scruples suddenly seemed feeble.

Just then I noticed that the malarial soldier had stood up and was clinging to a tree trunk. His whole body was trembling and he swayed to and fro. He was looking right beyond us, in the direction of the bluish, hazy fields. I followed his line of vision, but there was nothing special to see.

"What's wrong?" shouted the one-potato soldier. "Do you like the view over there or something?"

The soldier turned round, as if to see where the voice had come from, but he seemed unable to focus his eyes on any of us. I noticed a stain spreading down his trouser legs. Malaria had made him incontinent.

A couple of us walked over to him and put our arms round his body. I could feel its heat through his uniform.

"It's a damned nuisance," said one of the soldiers. "We can't change his trousers."

"It can't be helped. . . ." said another. "Hey, whenever you want to leak, just tell us. We'll help you stand up."

We laid him down carefully on the grass and returned to where we had been sitting.

"It's no use," said one of the men. "He won't last much longer."

There was a pause.

"Look here," said another soldier in an unexpectedly loud voice. "Do you realize you're all just a bunch of deserters?" He was the only man among us who still belonged to a company. No one answered.

I got up and set off for the spring about a hundred yards away by the foot of the mountain. I wanted to fill my canteen before it was too dark. As they saw me leave, several of the soldiers shouted to me asking if I would fill their canteens also. In the end, my arms were full of canteens. So even doomed men, I reflected as I trudged through the forest, cannot resist sparing themselves by exploiting other people's labor.

On my way back, I passed Yasuda. He had hung his mess tin over a fire and was bending over it. In the dark of the forest the flames lit up his face and I noticed that it was lined with countless wrinkles, like little gashes.

🏴
🏴
🏴 6 🏴 *NIGHT*

The slender moon followed the sun's halo, as if attached to it by a thread, and together they sank beyond the western mountains. It was pitch dark. We lay down, covering ourselves with our raincoats and using our haversacks as pillows.

Now the fireflies appeared in all their brightness, flying down the little streams that pierced the valley. Some of them darted straight ahead like rockets about two yards off the ground, while others flitted dizzily up and down describing the outlines of the trees. Finally they all gathered on one and lit it up like a great Christmas tree.

The malarial soldier was moaning. It was a regular moan and followed the exact rhythm of his breathing, as if to remind us all of the necessity of inhaling and exhaling.

"Hey, Dad, are you asleep?" said a voice near by. I recognized it as coming from the young soldier to whom I had not given any corn that evening. At first I thought that he was talking to me and I raised my head; but it was Yasuda who answered.

"What do you want?"

"Look, Dad, what do you really think is going to happen to us?"

"For God's sake, stop bothering me!" said Yasuda. "You've been asking me that ever since we left camp. How many times do I have to tell you—we'll just have to wait and see."

"That's all right for you. You're lucky. You know how to manage. But I . . ."

"Well, you'd better figure out some way to manage, too," said Yasuda.

"But how? I don't have a whole lot of tobacco like you. And how am I going to get around with this beri-beri?"

"You can get around better than me! You ought to be out in the fields seeing what you can pick up. That's how to manage. You don't think I'd be toadying here to these damned orderlies if it wasn't for my ulcers? No, I'd be out there in the fields hunting for food."

"Do they hurt—your ulcers?"

"They hurt like hell!"

"I'm sorry, Dad. But it's all right—I'll stick by you."

"Don't worry about me," said Yasuda. "If you think you're going to get some potatoes out of me by hanging around here, you're crazy! Why don't you go off by yourself somewhere and find your own food?"

"I'd be lonely."

"Don't be a damned idiot. How old are you anyway?"

"Twenty-one. I was called up last year. They graded me 2-B in my physical."

"If you're twenty-one, you're of age—so try to behave like you were! When things get like this, it's each man for himself. It's no good worrying about others. And I'll give you another tip—people can live on just grass and leaves for a whole month, sometimes even two months. And then . . ."

"Yes, and then what happens?"

"Well, something happens. Don't be such an idiot. Why look that far ahead?"

"It's different for you, Dad. You're older than me and you've got plenty of guts. But I've got to the point where I only want to die."

"All right, if you want to die, who's stopping you?" said Yasuda after a pause.

"Look, Dad, would you like to hear my big secret?"

"What's the use? It's got nothing to do with me."

"Seriously, I'm going to tell you something I've never told anyone before in all my life. My mother—she was just a maid in my father's house. She wasn't his wife at all."

"Is that all? There's nothing so unusual about that."

"Well, I've never heard anyone else say their mother was a maid like that."

"Most people don't go around bragging about it like you. But you can certainly read about it or see it in the films any day of the week."

"Yes, I know. I went to see *The Mother Whom Once I Knew*. But I got so fed up I had to leave halfway through."

"What the hell made you tell me all this now in the middle of the night?"

"Nothing special. I just wanted to get it out of my system. . . . Well, Ma got thrown out of the house after I was born. I stayed on, but no one told me anything about it. Then when I got older and started acting a bit wild, the old woman—Father's real wife, I mean—came out with the whole story."

Yasuda grunted.

"Wild, eh? What did you do?"

"Oh, nothing special. I used to hang around the tea-houses with my friends and go to the movies. Sometimes we went to the *pachinko* parlors."

"What's your father's business?"

"He's a blacksmith. He's got a shop next to the police-box on Shirokawachō in Tokyo. . . . Well, when the old woman told me, I got angry and ran away from home.

Then I got a job as a waiter in a place I knew. I also worked as a cook."

"Well, what's wrong with that?" said Yasuda. "If a fellow can stand on his own two feet and make a living, what does it matter who he's the son of?"

"But you see, I wanted to meet my real mother."

"Where was she?"

"She'd gone back to her home town in Chiba and got married. Father gave me her address and I went to visit her in Matsudo."

"I see."

"Her husband was an umbrella-maker and she lived in the shop. Luckily he was out. When she saw me, she gave me hell! She said I was a bastard and asked how I dared to come to her home like that. She said my father had no business giving me her address. She was in a real rage, I can tell you."

"Yes, the same old story," muttered Yasuda. "I still don't see why you had to tell me now."

"Well, I got angry too. So I ran away without even answering her."

"You seem to enjoy running away," said Yasuda. "So then everything was all right, wasn't it?"

"When I got back to Tokyo, I went to the movies. That's when I saw *The Mother Whom Once I Knew*. I couldn't stand it, though. I had to leave in the middle."

"I suppose you were crying."

"No, I was too unhappy to cry. I just got up and ran out."

There was a long silence. Finally Yasuda said: "Well, I might as well tell you my own story."

"Yes, please do. Was your mother a maid, too?"

"Of course not. It was the other way around with me—I'm the one that had the child."

"How?"

"I made a waitress pregnant while I was still at school. My old man found out about it and wouldn't even let me see the boy when he was born. I suppose I was rather a sap about the whole business. I let my elder brother take care of everything. He had the kid farmed out and saw that he had a proper education. He never breathed a word about it to anyone—not even to me. I had no idea what had happened to the kid. When I finished school, my old man found me a job in the country and I had to leave Tokyo."

"Did your brother have kids of his own?"

"Yes, but not till later. Until the old man died he just looked after this kid of mine. He kept him boarded out the whole time. Then, when the old man kicked the bucket, my brother brought the boy to the house and told me it was my kid. But he made me promise never to recognize him officially as long as I lived."

"Then you got married, I suppose."

"That's right. But that kid of mine, you know, he was a smart youngster—a damned sight smarter than my brother's own children!"

"What about your legal children?"

"Oh, he was smarter than them too!"

"How old is he now?"

"Sixteen. He's joined up with the Junior Air Force."

"Really?"

"Just before I came overseas in March, I went to see him at his camp. It's a funny thing, you know. I didn't think of wishing him good luck or anything, but just as I was leaving, the young fellow says to me: 'Take care of yourself, Dad.' "

"You're a bad parent, you know."

"Well, it's too late to do anything about it now. Anyhow, he seems to have turned out all right. He volunteered of his own accord for the Junior Air Force. For all I know, he may be flying somewhere up there this very minute. . . . Considering how he was born, I sometimes wonder if it wouldn't be best if he . . ."

"Don't say that! I know what you were going to say— it'd be best if he got killed. But you mustn't say it.

You're an evil person, you know. And you'll be pun-
ished for it one day."

"You're damned right I will! I'm going to die like a dog
—right here on this filthy island!"

There was a sound of subdued sniffling.

"For God's sake, don't cry," said Yasuda. "I can't do
anything about it now, can I?"

"I know, but when I hear about bad parents like you,
I can see why I've had such a rotten time of it myself. I
suppose my own Ma and Dad think I'd be better off dead
too."

"That doesn't necessarily follow," said Yasuda. "Anyhow, for God's sake stop that damned sniffling! You
aren't the only one here who's going to die."

"You're an evil person."

"Well, if I'm so evil, you can go to hell!" said Yasuda
with an air of finality. But a little later I heard him murmur: "Yes, I suppose that's how it'll happen. I'll die here
on this island with that son of mine."

At that moment one of the soldiers let out a deep sigh.
I realized that until then I had never heard the voice of
unadulterated despair. It was a low, rather thick sound,
dry and echoless, and it trailed off gradually. So inhuman
was this primitive statement of despair that I could not
possibly tell from whom it came.

"Look here, young fellow," I heard Yasuda say, "you'd better stick with me. I'll see that you get along all right."

"You really mean it, Dad? But . . ."

"But what?"

"You frighten me, you know."

"We'll stick together, I tell you. But that means you've got to work. Tomorrow morning we'll both go to the hospital and see if we can't get some odd jobs to do—carrying water, cleaning the mess trays—any damned thing. They'll be sure to give us at least one spud each if we work all day. D'you understand?"

"Yes, I understand, but—but can I do that sort of work with my beriberi?"

"Of course you can, you stupid fool!" said Yasuda. "It doesn't matter what work you do, so long as you do something."

Then their voices sank to whispers.

I lay back and reflected on how strange it was that among the bestial residue of a defeated army there should still be scope for a drama like this in which the cynical seducer of a café waitress took under his wing the timid bastard son of a maid. What, I wondered, would happen in the course of the next weeks and months, when conditions were bound to become still worse, to this peculiar pair who had so quickly adopted the relationship of father and son? By a strange combination of circumstances, I was to know only too well their extraordinary fate.

As I tried to go to sleep, the happenings of the eventful day began to flit through my mind. One by one the images lit up and then faded out: the moist lips of my squad leader when he had slapped me, the narrow eyes of the quartermaster sergeant, the frightened look of my companions here by the edge of the forest. They were like reflections thrown on a screen, and I looked at them without any particular feeling. This cool, detached attitude toward my own experiences was no doubt ideal for someone in my predicament.

Finally there appeared the image of the fires on the plain. My somnolent brain twisted the scene around freely behind my dark eyelids, until what I saw was a parched sky as a back-cloth and in front, the smoke of the prairie fires across the river, rising in intermittent puffs like the steam from the funnel of an old-fashioned locomotive. The smoke on the hilltop rose to a certain height, then curved at right angles to form a large hook; the curved end quivered uneasily like the needle of a compass. I was not afraid. I knew that this vision was the prelude to sleep, and, sure enough, I dozed off almost at once.

I was awakened by a noise. It was dark all around. From the direction of the hospital I could hear a voice shouting abuse and at the same time something that sounded like a wet cloth being beaten against a wall. It took me some time to realize that it was the sound of a face being slapped. The door of the office was thrown open and candlelight poured into the black night. A man stumbled out of the room. He had a large welt on his forehead. Clearly the one-potato soldier had been caught trying to steal food and had received his punishment. "We'll all be chased away from here tomorrow," I thought, and fell asleep again.

𝕎
𝕎
𝕎 7 𝕎 *THE ROAR OF GUNS*

When I awoke again, it was to the sound of heavy firing. It was almost daylight. By the river in the west the air was full of noise and smoke. The mighty concatenation of explosions approached our forest and seemed to fuse the whole surrounding sky into a narrow strip. The roar of guns grew terrifyingly close, and with it came a bellowing rumble as of distant thunder. Beyond the hills that I had crossed the day before I could see a single reconnaissance plane flying round in small circles, like a bird of prey watching for its victim. The bombardment seemed to be concentrated directly below the plane.

We all jumped to our feet. The doctors and orderlies hurried out of the hospital and peered beyond the hills.

Suddenly there was a whistling sound of a shell, and a moment later a huge cloud of smoke arose on the plain where yesterday I had seen the prairie fire. Someone gave an order and the doctors and orderlies dashed into the hospital, to re-emerge at once with their rifles and field equipment. They came running toward us at full speed.

The range of shellfire was reaching steadily over the hills in our direction. The medical personnel rushed past us toward the valley, as if they could possibly outstrip the rapidly expanding range of the shells. A few of our group followed them. The one-potato soldier with the great welt on his face took advantage of the confusion to run back to the hospital; even the roar of the shellbursts could not deflect him from his determination to steal food. The patients began to pour out of the wards and scatter about helplessly, each going his own way.

The malarial soldier was lying face-down on the grass without moving. I tapped him on the shoulder, then realized that he was dead.

I walked alone into the forest toward the spring where I had gone to fetch water the night before. When I reached the mountain range, I decided to climb the foothills and make my way along them, parallel to the broad front from which the shellfire was coming.

After scrambling about sixty yards up the zigzag path, I reached a turning from where I had an unbroken view of the whole valley. I stopped and looked down. The patients who had fled from the hospital had by now exhausted their strength and were lying motionless, scattered like little beans between the ridges of the cornfields.

The roar of guns continued, but so far the shells had not quite reached the hospital compound. I wondered where the main firing could be coming from. This was clearly not one of the usual trench-mortar bombardments. No, it was probably a softening-up from one of the American warships offshore, preceding a concerted landing operation on the west coast. After all, we were separated from the sea by less than three miles of flat, open plains.

Smoke began to rise from one of the hospital buildings. It whirled around in little eddies, curling up from under the eaves, and finally formed a single thick, convoluted column. Through the windows I could make out a red glare. Had the orderlies fired the buildings, according to normal army practice before abandoning a position? Or had the predatory one-potato soldier dropped a match or upset an oil lamp by mistake?

I noticed that the main group of soldiers, who had been running to the left, had now slowed down to a walk and were heading for the protection of a hill that stood by itself in the valley. From the bald summit of this hill rose a thin line of smoke; it wavered in the early morning breeze, then gradually grew stronger. It was a smoke signal.

The roar of guns stopped. The hospital had now become a thick bundle of flames. From within the furious blaze came a swishing sound like that of running water. The column of smoke rose compactly to about the level of the hill on which I was standing and then opened up like a fan.

My duty was clear: I should return to the valley and help my wounded comrades who had fallen under the bombardment. But my impulse at this moment was far removed from such heroism. To my amazement, I realized that all I wanted to do was to laugh. The sight of my companions running about helter-skelter like insects as they tried to fly the fury of unseen enemies struck me then as unspeakably funny. What earthly concern could they be of mine?

I burst into laughter and, still laughing uncontrollably, turned my back on the wounded soldiers and continued up the mountain path. I might have cut a rather more gallant figure had I been climbing this mountain for some other purpose than to save my own skin.

The entire central mountain range now spread out ahead of me under the glowing morning sky—the mountain range that at this very moment was being looked at from thousands of different angles by the thousands of soldiers on Leyte Island as they faced their imminent deaths. From where I stood, its silhouette was like the humps of a camel's back.

A strange force drove me on. I knew full well that only calamity and extinction awaited me at the end of my journey; yet a murky curiosity impelled me to continue plumbing the depths of my own loneliness and despair until the moment when I was to find death in the corner of some unknown tropical field.

❧
❧
❧ 8 ❧ *THE RIVER*

Day after day, night after night, I wandered aim-
lessly through the hills. The muffled roar of guns reverberated constantly in the surrounding mountains and
fields, and enemy planes shot past overhead; but I saw
no one. I gathered that I must be in the very middle of
the triangle formed by the three strategic points of
Burauen, Albuera, and Ormoc; and here, as in the
center of a cyclone, it was strangely calm.

One day I awoke at dawn to the thunder of guns in
the northwest and, looking across the hills, saw blue and
red flares crisscrossing each other in mid-air like fire-
works. That night I watched brilliant lights describing
the outline of the town of Ormoc, where my company
had previously been based. Evidently the Americans
had now landed on the west coast, our only remaining
position on Leyte Island.

My food had given out some time before, but I could
not tell whether I had actually begun to starve. The
reality of my impending death superseded all else. My
body was numb; only the back of my head seemed to be
awake and resonant.

I was utterly free—free to live these days as I wanted, and free also, thanks to my hand grenade, to choose the exact moment of my death. As I trudged from one deserted hilltop to another, with the great mountains stretching monotonously to my left, piled one on the other in a continuous series under the burning tropical sun, I knew that these were simply hours of grace that I was bestowing on myself.

One afternoon, the grass bow of the hill curved sharply downward and I descended into a lonely ravine where a dry gully twisted its way between the roots of bare trees. The ravine itself sloped down, forming a sort of funnel with the bordering hills; it came to an end at the top of a low cliff, and below I could see water gushing out.

I realized that I was thirsty and clambered down the side of the cliff. The water spurted out of a hole in the rock to form a clear, round pool about six feet across. I lay down by the edge and drank the cool water to my heart's content.

The water flowed out of the pool into a narrow rivulet, then into another pool, and beyond that into a wider stream. A path followed the water downstream and I walked along it. The rippling murmur gradually became more insistent and the path crossed the stream.

The ever-widening flow of water left the path and slid
into a dark forest. As I followed the path around the edge
of the forest, I could hear the sound of a waterfall growing louder and louder through the trees. Then the sound
receded. Suddenly the stream splashed its way out of the
forest and once more began to run beside the path.

Ahead of me was a dense grove of bamboos. The sun
glittered through their straight trunks onto the wall of a
rock formation. Beyond this lay yet another sloping valley. The stream had now turned into wide rapids, which,
after pouring through the bamboo grove, foamed down
the valley over the pebbles.

The sun gleamed on the river's surface, and clouds
scudded across the dazzling sky to disappear over the
mountain peaks. On the sloping banks of the river bamboos grew luxuriantly, their green leaves wafted by the
breeze. Driftwood, which remained from the floods of
the rainy season, lay drying on the sand and pebbles of
the river's edge. Now and then the water would strike the
banks capriciously, or form deep pools, or spread out
into frothy rapids. In the evenings by the shadows of the
pools I could hear the river deer cry as they came down
to drink, and at dawn the turtledoves cooed high on the
river bank.

One evening the path climbed the bank and led me into

a grove where great creepers stretched out in tangled mazes. As I lay down to sleep I noticed that the earth mound that I had chosen for my pillow was gleaming wanly. I scooped up some of the earth and it shone in my hands like a firefly. It must have been the phosphorescence remaining from the carcass of some animal who had died in this place.

The next day I rejoined my river and came to a place where, under the shadow of a great hanging tree, the water swirled around in torrents between huge boulders. I took off my boots and stepped into the foam. My insteps were emaciated and my feet looked shriveled like a chicken's; it hurt as I immersed them in the water. I looked at my hands. Here, too, the skin was stretched tightly over the bones; the flesh had receded and my fingers looked almost twice their normal length.

Death was no longer an abstract notion, but a physical image. Already I could see my dead body lying here on the riverbank, with the stomach blown out by my hand grenade. Soon it would decay and be resolved into its various elements. I knew that my flesh was composed two thirds of water: before long that water would begin to flow—yes, it would merge with this very river and flow downstream.

I gazed into the river before me. The water hurried

along with a secret whispering sound that reminded me of my childhood. It crossed over stones, made little detours, then vanished into the distance. Constantly more water appeared from behind; there was no end to its flow.

I sighed. My consciousness would certainly cease the moment that I died; but my flesh would blend with the river and remain part of this great universe. Such would be my survival.

What made me so sure of this survival was the fact that the water was *moving*.

🚩
🚩
🚩 9 🚩   *THE MOONLIGHT*

More days and more nights passed and still I saw no one. When I had left my company the moon had been only three days old; now it was almost full. At nightfall it would suddenly peep from across the summit of the mountain range; then it would glide across the narrow stretch of sky to hide behind the mountains opposite. For a long time after it had disappeared, its light would linger over the valley. The unchanging, cosmic motion of the moon seemed to mock me in my transience.

One evening the hills on the left of the valley broke off, and I could see another valley stretching out in the distance. Here, too, flowed a mountain stream. It joined my own rapids and together they made a wide river. In the triangle formed by their confluence grew a clump of palm trees.

I stood under the trees and looked up through the foliage to where the coconuts nestled in their roundness, like clusters of babies' heads. Here at last was food in abundance! But I realized at once that I was by now far too weak to climb the tall trunks.

The hard, fan-shaped leaves clattered in the wind. I lay down on the grass under the trees, closed my eyes, and listened. Now I knew that I was starving. I picked a handful of grass and chewed the roots. The inside of my mouth was numb.

At night the sky shone indigo-blue between the leaves of the palm trees, and high above, the cool, round moon made the ends of the leaves glitter like swords.

Was this, I wondered, to be the end? Was I now to suffer the agonies of starvation, even as I lay looking up at the masses of fruit with their fragrant juice and succulent flesh? Was I to linger here, clinging ignominiously to this tree trunk, until I drew my last croaking breath?

No, I must leave this place while I still had the power to choose my actions. The moon-drenched sky had suddenly filled me with a new yearning. Perhaps it was merely a final access of the instinct to survive. Yet it was a familiar feeling, which I had often experienced in the halcyon days of my past. How many times had I not gazed up at such a sky with this same yearning?

I searched my memory for these past occasions, but they eluded me. Then I realized that the palm trees which surrounded me were being transfigured. Gradually they were turning into the various women whom I had known and loved in the past. The young palm tree with its lifted leaves which stood there like a dancer was the girl who had left me without yielding to my love. That shadowy tree, with its heavy, dropping leaves that looked like tresses, was the older woman who had suffered because of her love for me. And the tree next to it, which proudly radiated its leaves in all directions—yes, that was the high-mettled woman who, though we had both loved each other, had refused ever to confess this love, even to herself, and in the end had broken away from me. Now all these women had gathered here in the moonlight to witness my final hours.

I recalled afresh the various moments in which I had

shared pleasure with them. I remembered that the thighs of one woman had been no thicker than the arms of another. . . . Yet in my present moribund state I could not bring to mind the actual taste of pleasure, but only the craving that preceded it.

The yearning in which the moonlit sky had engulfed me was like the craving that I had felt for some woman whose body and spirit were unattainable. And I now perceived that it was just because the sky was likewise unattainable that I so yearned for it. It was not because I was still alive that I clung to the notion of life, but because I was already dead.

This paradoxical conclusion had one comforting aspect: if I no longer belonged to the world, I at least did not have to undertake to kill myself. I smiled with satisfaction. Then I fell asleep.

🎟
🎟
🎟 10 🎟 *THE CROWING OF THE COCK*

Two days and nights I lay under those palm trees. Then I left. It required an immense effort to stand up, but once I was on my feet my legs seemed to move forward of their own accord.

My eyes kept scanning the trees for coconuts. As I trudged through a wood that overlooked the river like a grandstand I peered into the thick foliage where those round pendants might be lurking. It was useless. The mad, luxuriant, tropical green reflected nothing but the glare of the sunshine. I smiled to myself as I remembered how I used to picture the blessings of nature in these lands of permanent summer.

I returned to the path by the river and followed it farther downstream. The water sparkled now over great brown rocks. By the shore a black oily liquid oozed out of the ground, trickled along reflecting variegated patterns of red and blue and green and yellow, then sank into the sand.

The river grew still wider and a grass plain stretched out on both banks. Clusters of sparkling reeds grew like little groups of people. They had taken root in even the minutest mounds of dry ground by the river bed. Their delicate cilia, blown off by the wind, hovered playfully about the ears of the plants before being wafted away into the distance.

A hill stood by itself next to the river. All the way up its narrow slopes, rushes crawled like a horse's mane.

Somehow the contour of the hill reminded me of a woman's *mons Veneris.*

I started walking along a path that climbed straight up following the line of the rushes. The path was dug about six inches deep into the red clay of the hill, revealing the dense roots of the grass on both sides. On one bank of the path I noticed a series of regular indentations, obviously made by a shovel. The sudden traces of a human implement in this deserted valley astounded and frightened me.

Just then I heard a cock crow. Its wild cry echoed from the top of the hill, rending the peaceful afternoon air. The marks of a shovel and the crowing of a cock—together they could only point to the presence of Filipinos, to that presence which always lurked in these islands, waiting to chastise us invaders. Yet I continued climbing.

At the top of the hill the row of rushes came to an end, and a saddle-shaped field stretched as far as a thicket of tall, dark trees. From among the trees I once more heard the harsh cry of the cock.

The path cut its way through the field and reached the thicket. Here, in the green shadow of the leaves, stood two logs, one on each side of the path, like gateposts. When I passed them, the path divided into two forks, which curved symmetrically, as in a formal garden. Beteen them was a plot of grass and beyond this the sun shone through.

It was utterly quiet. I peered through the trees and saw a cabin. This is where the chickens must be, I thought—and the people. For a moment I hesitated. Then, firmly grasping my rifle, I stumbled through the thicket, as if being pushed from behind, and emerged into the open.

An unexpected scene awaited me. The cabin stood by itself with its back to the edge of a steep slope. Down the slope, for more than a mile, the ground was covered with huge tree trunks, which lay about in all directions. At the bottom of the slope I could see a small hollow; opposite this, another slope, likewise covered with tree trunks, crawled upward until it disappeared into a wood.

There was no one in sight. Several chickens were perched on a tree whose slender, elliptical, reedlike leaves fluttered just above the roof of the cabin. They were the scrawny black chickens indigenous to the Philippines. Evidently they were still quite tame, for when I approached they clucked back and forth to each other for a few moments, then turned their profiles to me and stood there quietly.

Suddenly they appeared to me like birds of paradise.

Perched there neatly, each on one of the branches that stretched out alternately in opposite directions, they did not seem to be creatures of this world.

My next thought, however, was less poetic: I decided to catch one of them. I was well aware that these birds, unlike our plump Japanese chickens, were very good fliers. I sneaked up carefully, hoping to take them unawares, but before I could stretch out my hand they had all flown off and alighted on a distant patch of earth.

I lay down, leveled my rifle, took careful aim, and fired. The chickens flew off at a steep angle like gliders, and landed far down the slope. Then they ran farther away, cackling raucously to each other.

Another gloomy prospect opened before me. Just as earlier my physical weakness had condemned me to lie unavailingly under the fruit of the palm trees, now, because of being a bad shot, I was to starve here in the presence of all these chickens.

I watched them as they strutted down the slope, no longer paying the slightest attention to me. Now and then they stopped unconcernedly to peck at something on the ground.

Suddenly it occurred to me that this very pecking might be the clue to my reprieve. I rushed down the slope, dodging between the roots of the trees and their felled trunks. But I did not even have to go as far as the chickens, for what I now found growing everywhere between the tree roots were the long stems of Philippine "potato trees" and the trailing leaves of "vine potatoes." The large tubers grew underground. I pulled one of them out, quickly wiped off the dirt, and bit into it. The dry, flaky potato crumbled between my teeth and I swallowed. I had to eat several before I could taste even the slightest sweetness. Only then was I able to take some of them down to the spring in the hollow to wash the dirt off properly.

I lay down and drank. The water gushed out between the rocks to form a rivulet that was covered by a thin membrane of volcanic ash. I noticed that twigs had been piled up along the banks. At the bottom of the water were leaves and stems that I recognized as taro.

Clearly I had stumbled on a well-cultivated Philippine plantation. That I should have done so in this area where our scattered troops had so long been foraging for food was little short of miraculous. Had I been Robinson Crusoe, I should at this moment have thrown myself on my knees and offered up thanks to God. Even from an Oriental infidel like myself, the occasion seemed to demand thanksgiving. But I did not know to whom I might give my thanks.

Next, I found enormous Philippine beans growing to the height of bushes. Their brown, hatchet-shaped pods had burst open and inside nestled tiny black grains; these no doubt were what the chickens had been nibbling on the ground. Other plants contained red grains that looked like Indian strawberries and tasted like tomatoes.

When I had eaten my fill, I walked up to the cabin. It was supported by the usual bamboo props, and its roof was thatched with reeds. There was a heavy smell of dust. The dirt floor had been raised in one corner to provide for a crude oven; next to it were stacked a few pieces of earthenware. The cabin boasted of no furniture except one flower-embroidered cushion lying on the floor. I made this incongruous cushion into my pillow and instantly fell asleep.

⚑
⚑
⚑ 11 ⚑ *INTERLUDE IN PARADISE*

I spent the next days eating to my heart's content. The echo of firing from the surrounding hills became sporadic, and in the south the shooting seemed to have stopped entirely; no doubt our forces in that area had been wiped out. I imagined the forests down in the valleys filled with the corpses of Japanese soldiers. It gave me an uncanny feeling to visualize these scenes of carnage while I lived here in my paradise. I am not sure that in some strange way I may not actually have been hoping for the death of my comrades, knowing that beyond this interlude of satiety my own death awaited me.

However, it looked as if the interlude would last for some time. There were still over twenty "potato trees" below the cabin, and on the opposite slope I could make out many more stems, covered with large leaves in the shape of basket hats. I was careful not to squander any of my new wealth. I cut the roots neatly with my bayonet, washed them in the stream, and peeled the skin. The only shortcoming of my paradise was that I had no fire and was obliged to eat everything raw. I tried to make up for this by chewing my food very carefully and, as a result, a considerable part of my day was spent on meals. However, despite all my precautions, I soon began to suffer from diarrhea.

The chickens were always gathering in a clucking mass outside the cabin, and at night they slept by the eaves. Often they walked right up to me. They had become my only friends and seemed to have forgotten completely my rude behavior on our first meeting. I used to observe them closely, and I discovered that they never blinked.

Yet I was bored in my new paradise. If this land had belonged to me, or if I had had the intention of living here all my life, I should have mustered my scanty knowledge of agriculture and contrived to renew the crops. But I was keenly aware of my transient status and could not bring myself to plan for the future.

At any moment, I realized, the Filipino owner might return. To guard against being taken unawares, I moved my daytime headquarters from the cabin to a spot in the forest whence I could survey my temporary domain without fear of discovery.

My only callers were American planes. Sometimes they flew past in formation, filling the sky above my paradise with their clear roar; more often they came singly. One morning a plane suddenly skimmed over the trees with an ear-rending screech. It was so close that I could clearly see the pilot. He was wearing a plain red scarf and, as he passed above me, he sat motionless in his cockpit, looking straight ahead like a doll. A certain feeling of human sympathy stirred within me for this American pilot, the first person I had seen in all the time since I had left the hospital. He was, to be sure, an enemy and a symbol of danger. But here in my new paradise I found something unconvincing in the idea of having enemies.

Among the many-pitched gunbursts and explosions that reverberated over the hills I could now and then make out the chugging of motors. It did not seem to come from an airplane, but sounded, rather, like motor-boats. This was my first inkling that I might be right next to the sea.

I tried to take my bearings. In my aimless wandering through the valleys after the hospital was bombarded, I must have walked about eight miles; accordingly, I was some twelve miles away from the spot where my company had been camped. From the direction of the sun I knew that I had been heading due north, and since my unit's position was twenty-five miles directly south of the Ormoc base I must have been about halfway between these points. The position of the polar star told me that the cabin was facing northeast; the opposite slope therefore faced southwest, that is, toward the sea.

So unenterprising had I become in my new-found satiety that I had never once bothered to climb the slope and examine the terrain beyond. I now hurried to make up for this lack of curiosity. I rushed down past my "po-tato trees," crossed the slippery moss-covered logs that formed a natural bridge high over the hollow, and scrambled up the opposite slope. Already I could feel a sea breeze on my cheek.

A moment later the sea itself lay before me. The rivulet twisted its way out of the hollow and debouched into the valley as it headed for the sea. The woods broke off at the foot of the hills and a mountain stream cut its way diagonally across the plain before disappearing into another clump of trees. Beyond these trees was a bay of calm water, bordered on both sides by imposing promontories.

The sound of the motorboat came from there; yet there were no boats in sight; the regular put-put-put of engines, echoing against the rocky promontories, reached across the plain and over the hills. I could not remember having seen this bay before. No doubt it was south of the point from where we had headed inland after our disastrous west-coast landing.

As the coast itself was hidden by the forest, I could not tell whether it was inhabited, but I felt reassured at having seen no houses. I took a last look round and started back for my cabin, wondering vaguely what the object might be that I had seen glittering above the green of the trees.

☙
☙
☙ 12 ☙ *THE SYMBOL*

Thereafter it became part of my daily routine to
walk across the logs, climb the slope, and sit there gazing
out to sea. The Visayan Sea was ringed in by close-lying
islands and was always calm. In the evenings I could
make out, behind the triangular islets that dotted the
water, the vast silhouette of the mountains on Cebu Island, where my company had formerly been stationed.
Crimson clouds radiated from above the peaks and
reached up to the zenith of the sky. As I sat watching, the
sea would gradually grow dark and Cebu become hazy
in the distance. Then I would trudge resignedly back to
the cabin.

In the mornings, the striped pattern of the waves
stretched out alluringly across the waters. But I had to
reconcile myself to my landlocked existence in the hills.

The object that projected above the forest near the
shore was most conspicuous in the evening, when it
glittered in the setting sun. From its shape and color, I at
first took it to be a withered branch; yet somehow it
lacked the natural quality that makes us judge something
to be part of a tree.

One day I strolled some fifty yards to the right of my usual position in order to view the object from a new angle. Observing it closely, I made out two prongs sticking out at a certain distance from the top. Suddenly I recognized the shape. It was a cross.

I shuddered with fear. Prolonged loneliness had by now made me easily frightened of anything new, and the sudden appearance of this religious symbol gave me an almost physical shock.

The cross no doubt decorated the top of a church, which was always the highest building in any Philippine village. On the other side of this forest, then, there must be a seaside village. Below the church there must be houses, and in these houses, people. As there were no American ships in the bay, these people could only be Filipinos. And however pious these Filipinos might be in their dealings with each other as they dwelt there in the shadow of the cross, their attitude to me could only be one of fierce enmity.

I felt not the slightest hatred for them; yet I knew only too well that since the country to which I belonged happened to be fighting the country to which they belonged, there could never be any human relationship between us involving the symbol that glittered above the trees. Indeed, because that cross was in the hands of my country's enemies, it was for me a symbol not of love, but of danger.

Yet I could not take my eyes from the cross. A single black plane moved slowly above it. The sun began to sink, and finally its light merged into a hazy blue that covered the whole sky. Only then did I leave my hilltop.

I spent that night thinking about the cross. In my present state of physical satiety and mental emptiness, in which I passed almost all my time eating in order to ward off an ineluctably approaching death, my heart accepted with eagerness this powerful human image.

The cross was to me a familiar thing. In my childhood this symbol of a foreign religion had penetrated even the smallest Japanese hamlet. At first I had approached it out of curiosity; then I had become fascinated with the romantic creed that it represented. But, later, an agnostic education had separated me from what I then came to regard as childish delusions, and I had begun to evolve a "system" that combined conformity to social demands and conventions, on the one hand, with a type of personal hedonism, on the other. This system was far from ideal, I well realized, yet it had served me well enough in my day-to-day life.

Now, in the loneliness of defeat, my "system" had inevitably begun to break down. My renewed fascination with the symbol of the cross was ample evidence of this. For the first time in years, I found myself wondering whether the ideas of my youth had, in fact, been mere illusions, and I tried to analyze my acceptance of an irrational belief in God's existence. No doubt my general ignorance and inexperience had been largely responsible; but I now remembered that there also had been another factor closely related to my personal development. I had sought a transcendent being, called God, because of the awakening within me of the irrepressible urge of sexuality; I had instinctively felt this urge to be evil, yet had realized that it could only be curbed by some powerful outer force.

"Love is pleasure taken in complicity." Though logically I may never have accepted the poet's pronouncement, I could well remember the sense of awe that these words had aroused in me. I could not help feeling that sexual love was bad, precisely because it was so agreeable. Later, of course, I had rejected all these ideas as mere adolescent aberrations, and I had never again suffered the slightest compunction about sexual indulgence.

Now, for the first time in years, my earlier doubts recurred, and with them a determination finally to think things out to a conclusion. If my adolescent feelings about the sinfulness of sexual pleasure had contained even the slightest particle of truth, then the rest of my rationalistic, pleasure-seeking life had been nothing but a web of errors. Where was truth—in my adolescent qualms or in my adult acceptance of hedonism as the guiding principle? It could surely not lie between the two.

I lay gazing at the dark ceiling of the hut, thinking; but I could come to no conclusion. Instead, I let my mind rest on memories of my youthful days, days that now seemed unbelievably tranquil, when I had believed in this foreign God, read the words of those sent by him, sung their psalms—and loved girls without desire.

When I awoke the following morning and saw the chickens perched on the tree near the cabin roof, busily clucking to each other, I realized that I was now looking at them in an utterly different spirit than when I had first arrived.

As usual, I went down the slope and pulled up a "potato tree." Suddenly this action seemed completely pointless. I left the root on the ground and hurried up the opposite slope. This morning the cross looked like a bird perched on the treetops. The short crossbar was spread out like a pair of wings and for a moment it looked as if it were going to plunge into flight.

It was then that the notion of going down to have a closer view of the cross first flitted through my mind. Immediately I realized what this would imply, and I almost doubted my own sanity. To go down to that church meant walking straight toward death at the hands of my enemies. Surely that symbol from my youth was not worth risking my life for, limited though that life might be!

As I gazed at the forest, my spirit torn between yearning and irresolution, the cross seemed to gleam more brightly. I told myself, in an access of clear-mindedness, that probably it was not a cross at all. But even as I looked, the unmistakable geometrical form became more and more prominent.

🐦
🐦
🐦 13 🐦 *THE DREAM*

That night I had a dream. I had already walked down into the village by the seaside. In the market place a row of shadowy shops displayed their multi-colored cakes and fruit. It seemed to be a feast-day, for Filipino men and women were ambling along in their finery, talking and laughing gaily to each other. Dangerous as my presence was for them, they did not seem to pay the slightest attention to me. It must have been because I was not carrying my rifle.

In an open square I came on a group of dancers performing on an improvised stage. The men and women all seemed to have an admixture of European blood. Their well-formed limbs twisted together as they danced, and frequently they would stop in various lascivious poses. It struck me as strange that there was no one but me watching them. Then I saw that the market place, too, was empty. Everyone must have gone to church.

The church was a rectangular building, constructed, like those I had seen on Cebu, in the style of a basilica. High above the rough façade was the familiar cross, but it now had a somewhat swollen appearance. I realized with dismay that I did not feel any of the expected excitement on seeing it close at hand.

I pushed the half-open door and walked in. The church was packed with people, all kneeling in prayer. A voiceless hum hovered over their bowed heads.

From the vestments of the Western priest who was saying mass at the altar, I knew that this was a funeral service. In front of the altar lay a coffin draped in black. The name of the deceased was inscribed in Roman script. I walked up the nave and read. It was my own name.

A biting sorrow seized my heart. So I was dead after

all. The "I" who stood here looking down at the coffin was no more than a spirit. That was why no one had noticed me.

I opened the lid of the coffin and gazed into my own dead face. It was a thinner face than that to which I was accustomed from the mirror and from photographs, and the cheeks were sunken. It looked like the faces of certain martyrs I had seen in Western paintings.

My hands were joined together over my breast. Clearly my dead body had been discovered in this pious attitude of prayer. It was for this reason that even my enemies were giving me a sacred funeral; this is why they were honoring me, a defeated Japanese soldier, as a saint.

Suddenly I felt uneasy. What virtue did I possess that I should be honored in this manner? Was I not, in fact, an impostor?

And, to be sure, when I scrutinized my face once more, I realized that this "corpse" was alive. My lips were red, as if bedaubed with rouge, and my closed eyelids were quivering. I was waking up in the coffin, and the only reason that I did not open my eyes was that I was feigning death. Now even that cool, sarcastic smile of mine which I knew so well had begun to play about my lips.

Then those lips spoke. *"De profundis,"* came my voice. *"De profundis clamavi."*

This was proof that I was still in the depths, that I was indeed no saint. Already the congregation seemed to have understood the imposture and I could sense them creeping up on me from behind. The hum of their voices swelled into a roar. Then the church bells began to toll: clang, clang, clang, clang—their clamorous shriek filled the air, drowning even the howls of the faithful. I felt a terrible pressure on my chest. . . .

I woke up. There was a buzzing sound in my ears, evidently the whir of an airplane crossing the night sky above me. I looked up at the red and green signal lights on the wings as they moved directly over the cabin toward the waning moon that hung in their path. For a moment the lights almost blotted out the shining reddish disk that encircled the moon; then they receded, to become small and dark in the moon-bathed sky. Finally I could only hear the distant hum of the motors.

Now I understood. It was foolish of me to linger here in the depths by myself until I died. I must go down into that church, even if it meant being killed, and resolve the religious doubt that had visited me at the end of my life. Perhaps this nightmare would prove to have been a revelation; perhaps, after all, I had a religious mission. If so,

I would throw myself on my knees in that cool church and pray.

Judging from the length of time between sunset and my falling asleep, there should still be ample time for me to reach the village before dawn if I left at once. I brushed aside a momentary sense of irresolution and stood up. As so often in my life, after vacillating between two courses of action I ended by adopting the more positive one.

I put some potatoes in the haversack and walked out of the cabin. My steel helmet and gas mask I left behind, but I decided to take along my rifle.

🦬
🦬
🦬 14 🦬 *THE DOWNHILL PATH*

My aerie was about one thousand feet above sea level and some five miles from the coast. I took the trail that ran from the top of the hill toward the cross. Presently I was in a wood. The moon broke through the trees, dappling with its sharp gleam the roots, which formed a series of natural steps. Now and then I could hear the feeble warbling of turtledoves, evidently tricked by the moonlight into believing that dawn was at hand.

I left the wood and continued downward through a moonlit field. The path, swollen with the black shadow of the grass, passed under the darkness of a grove, meandered along the sinuous edge of a cliff, crossed over a marsh, and circled a clump of trees. As I kept going down a feeling akin to joy rose within me.

After about a mile, I crossed a grass plain and entered a level wood where the path became wider. From within the moon-speckled trees I could hear the gurgling of water—a gentle, intimate sound like that of someone whispering behind a door. Ahead of me I could see a reflection shining more and more brightly through the leaves. I clambered down a red-clay slope and found myself on the banks of a wide river where the water glimmered over moss-covered rocks as large as millstones. The trees opposite grew right up to the water's edge.

I sat down on a trunk and drank from my canteen. I was relieved to have reached flat country after my long weeks in the mountains, but my relief was tinged with fear—the fear that a wild dog must feel as he approaches a human habitation.

After wading through the river across the slippery stones, I plunged on through the wood. The trees with their gleaming branches formed an imposing avenue. The path was now big enough for two people to walk abreast. It was a long time since I had seen so wide a path and I was frightened by the civilized impression that it gave.

Yet I forced myself onward. Now the trees became more and more distinct; I could clearly make out the speckles on their bark. Was it fear that had so sharpened my vision that I could distinguish these details deep in the night?

I emerged into another wide plain. The moon had become a huge, red, twisted orange hanging over the distant forest. Its weak glow was strangely different from the milky opalescence that now filled the surrounding fields. I understood the reason: it was already dawn. That was why the turtledoves had been warbling; that was why I had been able to see the bark so clearly in the forest.

Nervously I looked about, aware that something must have gone wrong with my calculations. Before leaving, I had concluded that I should reach the village in about two hours, in other words, well before dawn. I had now come to my estimated halfway mark at the edge of the original woods, and, to be sure, it had not taken me more than an hour. Yet here it was already full dawn. I must have made my mistake when I awoke from my dream and assumed from the moonlight that it was still the middle of the night.

Even as I stood by the edge of the forest the thick mist that had shrouded the fields was beginning to break up into insular patches. One large motionless patch on the right of the plain showed the location of the river. In the forest ahead the trees, which had first been hazy, now stood out clearly.

There were no houses to be seen, yet I could sense that I was approaching an inhabited area. Here in the tropics the mornings opened up suddenly, as if a curtain were being raised. Soon I would be exposed to all eyes, and I cursed myself for having embarked on such a hazardous venture. Yet I could not turn back at this stage; nor would my present state of mind allow me to wait by the forest till nightfall. I found myself scanning the tree-tops for the symbol that had led me into this danger, but now that I was on flat country, the cross was out of view.

I started to walk. In the fields, from which the darkness was lifting inch by inch, nothing moved but myself. My shoes were wet with dew and the soft squelching of their soles was the only sound. I walked on, as if being pursued by my own footsteps, and abruptly the feeling came over me that all this had happened to me before. To be sure, my reason told me that I had never walked like this through the uneasy dawn of a foreign land. Yet I *remembered* this very experience and tried in vain to identify it. Several times the memory seemed only a paper's thickness away from my consciousness. Somehow I could never quite seize it.

What I did recall in place of this elusive experience from the past was the fact that recently I had suffered time after time from such blockings of memory and that they belonged to what psychologists designate as "false recollection." This peculiar feeling of having experienced in the past what is happening now is always followed by failure to recall that past—for the simple reason, of course, that it never existed. According to Bergson, this phenomenon arises at moments of mental fatigue or prostration. At such moments, conscious life, which normally evolves without interruption, constantly feeding the memory with present experiences, ceases its advance, and the memory, no longer nourished with fresh material, strikes out on its own, as it were, ahead of one's consciousness.

Yet this lucid Bergsonian explanation struck me now as unsatisfactory. In particular, the hypothesis of a ceaselessly evolving life seemed untenable; for often I seemed not to advance, but to repeat myself or even to regress. Though the hypothesis was deeply satisfying to the modern rationalistic man, it was not satisfaction that I now sought, but positive truth. If one was ready to accept the premise of a constantly evolving life, would it not, I wondered, be at least as logical to believe in the guidance of some supernatural entity—in fact, in God?

As I walked along the plain, I felt certain that by probing within myself I could arrive at some more satisfactory explanation of "false recollection" than the mechanical theory that it resulted from a precedence of memory over consciousness at moments of mental exhaustion.

I now recalled the strange feelings that I had experienced some weeks before while walking through the forest after leaving my company. I had then been struck by the knowledge that I would never again pass the place where I was then walking. According to my conclusions at the time, the reason I was so moved by this knowledge was that I was anticipating my own death, and knew that I was no longer able to realize the fundamental premise of my normal life-feeling, namely the inherent assumption that I could *repeat indefinitely* what I was doing at the moment.

Granting that these conclusions were more or less correct, might it not be possible to explain my present feeling (that I had already done in the past what I was now doing) as a simple perversion of a wish that I might do it in the future? Might not one's mind, when it perceives that there is no possibility of repeating present experiences in the future, project these experiences into the past? In that case, the fact that "false recollections" appear at moments of fatigue or prostration need no longer be explained by any hypothesis that life has momentarily ceased its constant evolution; instead, it would indicate that at such moments, when the flow of one's everyday life is interrupted, the idea of being able to repeat what one is now doing (an idea that normally is taken for granted) emerges to the fore, and one's present actions are automatically projected into the past in order to make such repetition possible.

Now as I walked on, I was no longer worried by the rapidly ascending dawn. Everyone in the world, my past self included, lived under a constant illusion of repetition. Only I, as I headed toward death, no longer believed that I would repeat the present. This conviction lent me a new sense of daring.

15　*THE SIGNAL FIRE*

It was almost full daylight when I reached the forest ahead. I turned back and looked at the fields behind me. The sky had changed from madder-red to blue. In front of the cloud-swathed peaks of the central mountain range, the green foothills were beginning to emerge. Some brown specks high up amidst the green represented the paradise I had abandoned that night. I observed it now indifferently, as one might a former mistress.

Between the blanket of forest leaves the grass shone in the sunlight and the dew glistened. Some unfamiliar tropical bird warbled shrilly in the branches.

From my hilltop I had surmised that this forest must reach all the way to the village; but now it broke off and another plain stretched out before me, bounded on both sides by hills that rolled down to the bay. A river, spanned by a broken bridge, cut across the field.

I glanced swiftly about the plain. There were no people or houses in sight, but the bridge warned me that neither could be far off. In the marshland by the edge of the forest I saw two water buffaloes and, surrounding them, a flock of snow-white herons. Occasionally the herons would fly on and off the backs of the buffaloes; I noticed that one of them was pecking at its bearer and remembered having heard that herons were partial to certain insects that stick to buffaloes' backs, and that the buffaloes themselves were delighted to be thus liberated of the insects.

There was an ominous quality about this limpid early morning scene. I scrutinized each tree by the edge of the forest with the care of a professional sentry. For all I knew, one of those trees might be concealing my potential executioner. In a copse that bordered the hills on the left gleamed the white stem of a single fallen tree; its trunk pointed crazily toward the sky, and so clear was the morning air that from where I stood I could make out every single tendon of the roots.

I took my rifle from my shoulder-strap, and holding it at the ready, set out across the plain. A feeling of tension had gripped me—a feeling far removed from my recent serene speculations. Ceaselessly my eyes scoured the pellucid scene: I was determined to see my enemy before he saw me.

I reached the bridge. The river was turbid with the mud that it had gathered on its way through the marshes, and the water swirled sluggishly under the girders. Perhaps it was just at this point that my unseen enemy would strike.

Then a long, thin column of smoke began to rise unsteadily from the distant hilltop on my right. It was exactly like the smoke signal I had seen on the afternoon I left my unit, and suddenly I realized its true significance. The first prairie fire had heralded the bombardment of the near-by hospital, while the fire on the following morning had risen from the hill toward which the main body of soldiers was flying. Why had I only now grasped the connection between these fires and the ensuing disasters?

Yet I was not frightened. The Filipino sentries squatting by the foot of that distant column of smoke represented little danger compared to the inhabitants of the village whom I would in a few minutes be meeting.

I glanced around again. The heron perched on the buffalo's back lazily spread its wings and glided to the ground. As soon as its legs touched the humid earth, it began to beat its wings agitatedly; then it walked a few steps, folded its wings, and stood motionless by the edge of the forest.

From the opposite direction came the familiar chugging of engines. The American boats must have started their daily journeys out at sea.

Beside the soggy path, which now ran through a grove, water trickled along the exposed strata of rock. The trees were lined up on each side watching me. Suddenly the path veered to the left and began to go down a slope. Directly in front of me the whole village lay spread out.

🦋
🦋
🦋 16 🦋 *THE DOGS*

The slope fanned out and descended gently toward the sea. Down it ran a single road, bordered on both sides by some thirty palm-thatched huts. Through the cluster of palm trees at the bottom of the path I could make out the blue glitter of the water. There was not a sign of anyone on the road, and apart from the distant chug of motorboats, the village was deathly quiet.

The church stood a few yards away from the road, its white, narrow side rising above the row of huts. And there, to be sure, crowning the façade, gleamed a faded yellow cross.

On seeing that yearned-for symbol so close at hand, I felt my heart beat faster. The cross shone there above the village with a sort of barren, indifferent coolness. But this was not the moment to kneel down.

I leaned against a tree and waited for something to move. Time passed. The scene remained static.

From where I stood I examined the first hut on my left. The walls were filthy, the thatched roof seemed to be caving in, and some of the wooden steps that led to the front door were missing. I peered through the window, which was propped open by a stick; but there was no sign of life.

One might have thought that it was siesta time, instead of high morning, when even in a sleepy Filipino village like this one would have expected to detect at least some activity. There was no doubt about it: something here was radically wrong.

I ran to the first hut, bounded up the broken stairs, and stepped in. It was empty. In an open box in the corner of the room I could see some coarse pink underwear and a child's sandal. A fishing-net with weights was piled in a messy heap; on top of it lay an empty pack of Lucky Strikes, a wrapper from a chocolate bar, and a few other odds and ends.

The owners had obviously left in a hurry. Either they had taken their possessions with them, or the hut had subsequently been looted. But why should the Filipinos not have returned? After all, this area must now be more or less under American control. It became clear that the village was entirely deserted.

I ventured to show myself again in the open, and while I eyed the huts on both sides, began to walk slowly along the rough, empty road through the village. Now the puff-puff of the motorboat engines could no longer be heard, but a new sound came to my ears: a swishing sound, as of running water.

And then suddenly the air was filled with barking, and two dogs rushed at me full tilt from the side of the road. They stopped a few yards away and bared their teeth, barking savagely.

I felt grateful for my sturdy Army trousers. Aiming the muzzle of my gun in their direction, I quickly glanced about. The barking was loud enough to warn any near-by enemy of my presence, and at the time this seemed far more dangerous than the dogs themselves.

Still nothing moved. I turned back to the dogs. One of them was a terrier, the other a reddish mongrel of a type one often sees in Japan; their expressions were devoid of the gentleness that shows in the eyes of domestic animals. Now they were emitting low, ominous growls. I could feel their eyes fixed on the upper part of my body.

I kept my position and threatened them with my rifle. The animals, however, had apparently not been trained to fear firearms, for they did not flinch in the slightest as I took aim. At all costs I wanted to avoid shooting: I remembered the smoke signal on the near-by hilltop and was determined not to alert the Filipino sentries.

Without taking my eyes off the dogs, I lowered my rifle and, leaning it against my hip, quickly drew out my bayonet and fixed it into the muzzle. At that instant the red dog sprang at me, heading straight for my throat. My bayonet caught him in mid-air and slid between his ribs. The blood gushed out of his body as it fell to the side of the road.

The other dog was already in full flight. He rushed howling as far as the trunk of a palm tree down the road and then began to bark loudly. Dogs now joined him from various directions, and they stood in a pack by the roadside, barking together. I started to walk. Before I reached the dogs, they scattered to take refuge by the walls of the near-by huts; their wild barking seemed to fill the whole village.

I came to a small piazza. The façade of the church occupied one side. A black swarm of carrion crows perched on the sloping roof and on the arms of the cross. I was certain that the birds had not been there when I had looked at the cross before.

Now I could identify the swishing sound: it came from a hydrant opposite the church. White water was splashing out of a broken pipe that no one had bothered to repair. What could have happened in this village to keep the inhabitants from returning?

As I washed the blood off my bayonet it occurred to me how ironical it was that this weapon, which I had been given in order to destroy my country's enemies, should first have been used to slaughter a dog.

I wiped the bayonet, put it back in its scabbard, and then slowly drank from the hydrant. Although the water undoubtedly came from the mountains, it was free of the muddy flavor to which I had become accustomed: it tasted delicious. Yet it still lacked something I had been unconsciously longing for during the past weeks. What I really wanted was sea water—yes, it was the taste of salt, which I had not experienced for so long.

I ran past the palm trees, across the hard, brittle sand of the beach which caved in under my feet, and down to the sea. After wading into the water up to my knees, I filled my canteen and drank to my heart's content. Mixed with the longed-for saltiness, I detected a faintly sweetish flavor.

The calm surface of the Visayan Sea spread out before me. From the near-by promontory the cries of the cicadas bubbled forth, echoing across the water in a continuous high-pitched note only now and then interrupted by the sound of an American motorboat passing far out at sea.

The deserted beach described a smooth, white arc from the steep promontory on the right to a point on the left where a river notched its way through the sand as it flowed to its final destination. At the mouth of the river a wrecked sailboat lay with its bow buried in the river bed. Though this must be a fishing-village, no boat was to be seen.

A wind, with a moistness and a delicate scent that I remembered from the summer winds that had blown on the seashore at home, crossed the sparkling surface of the sea and, finding me standing there alone in the water, wrapped itself gently about me. Then it passed between my straddled legs and quietly continued its journey over the plains and mountains of Leyte Island.

After a while I realized the risk of exposing myself there by the shore and hurried back to the shelter of the palm trees. As I approached the village, I became aware of a sickly smell. It was a smell with which I was already well acquainted.

When my company had been camped in the south, we had occasionally managed to shoot cows wandering in the vicinity of our barracks; after we had eaten what was possible, we would abandon the offal in a near-by field. The huge carcass rotted almost at once under the tropical sun and only the head remained recognizable. For days after, our barracks were bombarded by the loathsome smell of decay—a sweet, pungent smell that seemed to assail our stomachs directly.

I realized now that this smell had been in my nostrils ever since I first entered the village. It had been there when I had run my bayonet through the dog and also when I had been drinking from the hydrant. Only when I had gone down to the sea had it temporarily lifted. Clearly the object from which the stench emanated was somewhere in the village. Perhaps it was the carcass of a pig abandoned by the inhabitants when they fled.

Soon I was standing once more in front of the church. The roof was still black with carrion crows. As I approached, they began to move about in a seething mass. One of them flew up sluggishly along the wall of the façade.

Just as in my nightmare, the cross failed to awaken the expected excitement. I noticed that it was dirty and that the gilt was peeling. The façade was stained with splotches left by the rain and the edges of the stone steps were broken. One of the two black wooden doors was half open, exactly as I had dreamt.

I felt exhausted and decided to rest in the church. I walked up the steps.

But I was prevented from going straight up.

᭞
᭞
᭞ 17 ᭞ *THE OBJECTS*

How could I have failed to notice the objects lying at the foot of those steps—objects that must have been in my field of vision for some time? My sense of perception must have already changed during the weeks since I had left my company. Clearly the link between my consciousness and the outer world was gravely attenuated. A solitary alien in enemy land, I had by this time come to notice only objects that warned me of immediate danger, or, as in this case, objects on which I literally stumbled.

I thought of them as "objects" though some might call them "people." In one sense, to be sure, they were people, but their bodies had already become mere dehumanized objects. What lay below those steps was corpses.

Having been corpses for some time, they had lost all the individual conformations of their past lives. Only their army trousers revealed some slight trace of the time when their owners had still belonged to humankind; yet even these were so discolored by mud and carrion slime that they no longer seemed like human clothing and were, indeed, barely distinguishable from the surrounding earth.

Even after I had recognized the objects as corpses I failed at first to see what really lay before me. I still trusted that I would find among this loathsome mess certain familiar human forms. But the grotesque trans-figurations of putrescence constantly deceived me.

The exposed arms and backs had swollen, in defiance of normal human proportions, to the utmost extent that the skin would permit; their surface gleamed a coppery red. From some of the bodies, intestines as large as thumbs protruded where the stomachs must have been. This presumably marked where the soldiers had been wounded; but there was no trace of any hole, for the swelling of the surrounding flesh bound the intestines tightly like sausages.

The heads too were bloated and looked as if they had been stung by thousands of hornets. Their hair, tightly glued to their skin by a liquid that had oozed out in the process of decomposition, made blurred borders on their foreheads. I knew then that I could never again look at the vague hairlines of wax dolls in shopwindows without a sense of horror.

Their cheeks bulged and their mouths were pointed. One might almost say that they had the expressions of pensive cats.

Some lay with their heads resting on the legs of their companions, others were contorted so that they hugged their own shoulders. The clothes over their buttocks were frequently torn and I could see the bare bones underneath. Now it was clear why this deserted town was so infested with dogs and carrion crows.

Why was I not overcome with nausea? At the time I had no such reaction. Perhaps nausea is simply an unconscious device of the egoist, who, when he hears of horrors outside the course of his present serene existence, allows only his stomach to respond.

What I did experience was a sense of desolation and a profound knowledge of betrayal. And what most moved me as I looked down at the carcasses of my former fellow soldiers, now bereft of all humanity, were the bent leg, the spread-out hand, the pointing finger—dumb tokens of their final human impulses.

Now at last I could surmise what had happened in this place. A group of Japanese soldiers had come to the village on one of their foraging expeditions. The inhabitants had taken the pillagers by surprise and slaughtered them. (A large meat cleaver next to one of the bodies suggested the instruments of their chastisement.) Later the villagers had left, fearing that Japanese troops, who, though no longer in control, were still marauding in the area in considerable numbers, might arrive and discover the massacre.

▶
▶
▶ 18 ◀ DE PROFUNDIS

I made my way around the corpses and climbed the steps. The interior of the church reflected no trace of the nearby horrors. Shafts of light from the high windows on both sides suffused a pleasant glow and illuminated the dust that had settled on the wooden floor and pews.

The font had been fashioned out of a large scallop shell, but the holy water had dried up.

On the walls between the windows hung a series of oil paintings depicting the Passion. At once I was struck by the profusion of red that the painters had lavished on their canvases, that is, by the goriness of their conception. The flogged back of Jesus was smeared with blood, and in picture after picture blood dripped from His feet and stained the wood to which He was nailed.

There was nothing original about these flat paintings; probably they were just copies of traditional compositions. Yet I realized that it was this very commonplaceness that most clearly bespoke the barbarism of the age in which they had been painted. At the same time I could not help wondering whether the people of old, who could worship amidst such a plethora of blood, had as they gazed at all that laceration of human flesh experienced emotions so very different from those I now felt.

On the altar stood a clumsy wax crucifix. The pale, naked body of Jesus had a corpselike tint, which contrasted with the reddish black of the coagulated blood. I carefully observed the figure of this good man who had been sentenced and executed some two thousand years before in a distant Roman colony. His hands were nailed, palms forward, to the ends of the crossbar at an angle of exactly forty-five degrees: clearly the force of gravity was pulling the body down and twisting the hands from their original position. . . .

What had happened to me? Here I stood facing the image that millions worshipped as the symbol of their faith, the image that had, indeed, been the object of my own infatuation—and all that I could see was a gory carcass being forced down by gravity. What dismal change had occurred within me?

I lay down in the dust of the floor and wept. Why, when after all these years I had again been stirred by religious feelings and even been drawn by them to this village, should I have been forced to see only the mangled corpses of my fellow soldiers and the tortured body of Jesus painted by some unskillful artist? Was it fate that had contrived this cruel jest, or did the fault lie within myself?

"De profundis!" The words I had heard from my own mouth in my dream the night before suddenly boomed through the church. They seemed to come from the choir loft and I looked up. But the church was empty. Who then could have called out those words?

It was my own voice, raised unconsciously in my agitation. If I have in fact become insane, it was then that my insanity started.

"Out of the depths have I cried unto thee, O Lord. Lord, hear my voice. . . ."

The great cry of appeal came back to me from my boyhood and fluttered in my heart. But in the decrepit Philippine church that my eyes mirrored as they peered around the ceiling there was no one, there was nothing, to answer me.

"I will lift up mine eyes unto the hills, from whence cometh my help."

The bond that linked my inner consciousness with the outer world had once for all been severed. There was nothing in that world which would ever answer my cry for help. Such was the fate to which I must abandon myself.

I stood up resolutely, and walking past a statue of the Virgin Mary, which made her look rather like a lady's maid, opened the side door of the chancel. Outside was a lawn overlooking the sea, and here I came upon still another corpse. The surrounding grass had dried up from the slime that oozed out of his decomposing body. One hand pointed in my direction, and I noticed that the nails were fantastically long. I vaguely wondered whether they had grown like that after his death, or whether they had already been long when he was killed.

Beside the lawn was a red-roofed presbytery. I pushed

open the broken glass window and entered the house. It had been thoroughly plundered. The cupboard doors were wide open, and the lids of the pots and pans had all been removed. Nothing was left except some books, among which I noticed two volumes of Edgar Wallace. "Why would a Philippine priest be reading detective novels?" I wondered.

It was high noon and outside the window the Visayan Sea brightly reflected the sunlight.

"They should build a hotel here for tourists," I thought inconsequentially. "It would be a great success."

I lay down on a rattan couch by the window. It gave me something of a nostalgic feeling to be stretched out again on furniture. Then I realized that I was hungry. I took a potato from my haversack and gnawed at it. It occurred to me that there might be a match in the house and that perhaps I should at last be able to eat something cooked.

I embarked on a scrupulous search of the presbytery. Undaunted by the traces of previous looters, I opened all the cupboards in the Western-style kitchen and examined the remotest recesses of the drawers, hoping that so insignificant an object as a match might have escaped their rapacity. It was useless.

Next I looked for a magnifying glass, with which I

might start a fire by concentrating the sun's rays. I imagined the priest as a rather elderly man who probably required a glass when he sat down to read his Edgar Wallace. I meticulously searched the study, but once again I was unsuccessful. Cursing this ill-equipped man of God, I lay down on a sofa and almost instantly fell asleep.

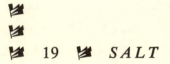

᭡ 19 ᭡ SALT

It was a long, painful sleep. When I awoke and looked out of the window, the pale, sad pink of the evening sun glowed over the sea. The sound of the motor-boats still echoed in the offing. I knew the risk I would be running if I stayed any longer in this enemy village, but I was too lazy to move. Then I must have dozed off again.

I could hear someone singing. It was a familiar Philippine song from which all the sensuality of the original Spanish melody had been winnowed, leaving only a residue of vague melancholy. The voice was a young woman's, and it came straight through the window as clearly as a beam of light. This could be no dream. I sat up and looked out.

It was already late at night. The water shimmered under the weak rays of the moon. The black shadow of a rowboat glided over the silver surface. Two people were in it; a man was at the bow and a woman was rowing. It was her voice, gently modulated by its journey across the water, that reached me through the window. Now and then she stopped her singing and laughed. I realized that I was gritting my teeth.

As the boat reached the shore the man jumped out and pulled it onto the beach. He stretched out his arm to help the woman from the boat, and then they both ran laughing across the sand, holding each other's hands.

Somehow I knew that they would come straight to this house. I lowered my head beneath the level of the window and strained my ears for the sound of their footsteps. Their laughing voices grew nearer. Then the back door opened and a moment later light filled the chink of the door that separated my room from the kitchen.

They were still laughing. My first thought was that they were lovers who had chosen this as a secret trysting place. But in that case why were they rummaging so long in the kitchen? Could they be servants who had formerly worked in the presbytery and were still keeping it in order for the priest's return?

I realized that at any moment they might burst into my room; and, sure enough, after a while one of them approached the door and the light through the chink vanished.

I stamped on the floor and instantly their voices stopped. Then I got up, pushed open the door with my rifle, and stepped toward them.

They stood close together and their wide-open eyes reflected the light of the oil lamp.

"Paigue ko posporo?" I said. "Can I have a match?"

The woman shrieked. It was a sound commonly described as a cry of distress, but in fact it was unconnected with any such human feeling as distress. It was a primitive, thoracic screech of fear.

Her twisted face was fixed on me, and still she let out her intermittent animal yelps. My immediate impulse was anger. I fired. The bullet must have entered her breast. A dark stain spread rapidly over the sky blue of her thin silk dress. She put her hand to her chest, rotated strangely in a complete circle, and fell forward.

The man shouted something, and raising one hand in front of his face, began to move slowly backwards. His retreating figure reminded me infuriatingly of Lisa in

Dostoevsky's *The Idiot,* and again I pulled the trigger. This time nothing happened. I realized that I had forgotten to load the gun, and I desperately fumbled with the breechblock. My hands had become hopelessly clumsy.

The man should have taken advantage of this delay to seize the gun barrel. Instead, the door slammed, and when I looked out of the window his figure was already retreating in the dark. I rushed after him as he dodged sinuously across the moon-drenched sand. A moment later he had reached the boat and started rowing madly out to sea. I knelt down and fired. The report of my rifle crossed the surface of the water, echoed against the distant promontory, and finally died away. The man frantically manipulated his oars. Already he was some distance from the beach. I laughed to myself and returned to the presbytery.

The woman's body had already begun to take on a corpselike quality. The breath hissed quietly out of her mouth like vapors rising from a marsh. I bent down and listened until the sound stopped.

Was it fate that had led me to this crime, or some terrible flaw in my own character? I did not know, but in any case I had to acknowledge that I was now no more than a brutish soldier who, far from being able to communicate with God, could not even mix with his fellow creatures. I had to scurry back to my solitary field in the mountains.

Before leaving, I was curious to discover what had tempted my victim to this fatal destination. I examined the kitchen and found that one of the floor boards had been removed. Below the floor lay an open canvas bag filled with coarse, dimly glowing crystals. These crystals were things of great value, both to those who still belonged to humankind and to myself. They were salt.

𝕸
𝕸
𝕸 20 𝕸 *THE RIFLE*

I stuffed my haversack with salt and left the house. The village was drenched with moonlight. As I hurried up the street the dogs started to bark. The harsh medley of their voices followed me from the shadows of the huts, and even after I was out of the village the noise still seemed to pursue me.

A gleaming mist hung over the fields like a curtain. Nothing moved. In the distance, under the adamantine night sky, rose the hills to which I was returning. Their surface was hazy and white like the powdered face of a woman, and they were as still as death.

I was overcome by sorrow. The image of the dead woman—her wide-open eyes, her little pointed nose, her breasts, her arm stretched on the floor as if thrown out in a moment of blissful passion—hovered constantly before my eyes.

It was not that I felt any particular regret. Homicide was now too common an occurrence to think of twice. Besides, it was by sheer accident that I had killed her: if she had not entered that particular house she would still be alive.

Why had I shot her? Because she had screamed. Yet while this may have been my immediate *motive* for pulling the trigger, it was not the real *cause*. I remembered that I had hardly aimed at all. It was simply by chance that the bullet had hit her breast. But if it had all been an accident, why should I feel so sad?

I reached the river that cut across the field near the forest. My boots clattered noisily across the wooden boards of the bridge. Halfway across, I stopped and leaned over the low handrail. I gazed into the water that flowed along, dully silvered by the moonbeams. Under the bridge countless eddies swirled round, changing their shapes, moving slightly downstream, and then returning to their original positions, as if pulled back by some magnetic force.

The recurrent motion of the eddies fascinated me. I realized that it was yet another example of that repetition which had played so important a part in my thoughts during the past solitary weeks.

Just as repetition was inherent in nature, so, I now realized, should it exist in human life. My life in the mountains had fitted into a regular cycle, but when I had come down to the village I had broken that cycle. As a result, I had killed an innocent Filipino woman. To be sure, it had been an accident; yet if the accident had arisen from my breaking a cycle, then I could hardly disclaim responsibility.

I stood up and held my rifle at the ready, just as I had done the day before when I had crossed the bridge in the opposite direction. Then I placed the butt of the rifle against my hip in exactly the position it had been in when I had shot the woman.

I looked down at it. The weapon shone with a sinister gleam. It was a 25-caliber rifle. It had been assigned to a school for training purposes, and the Imperial chrysanthemum crest on the cover of the breechblock had been crossed out with a large X; subsequently, with the growing shortage of weapons, the rifle had been retrieved by the Army.

I had a feeling of nausea and suddenly understood that my recent crime had depended entirely on this rifle. If only I had left it behind when I came down from my mountain, the woman could have screamed as much as she liked without the slightest danger.

It was my country that had forced this lethal weapon on me, and until recently my usefulness to my country had been in exact proportion to the amount of damage I could inflict with it on the enemy. The reason, however, that an innocent young woman now lay dead was that I had continued to carry the rifle even after I had been rejected by the Army and ceased to be of the slightest use to my country.

Without further ado, I dropped the rifle into the river. It disappeared below the surface with almost insulting rapidity, making a single gurgle as if to mock the plight of the solitary soldier who had impulsively discarded his only effective weapon. Then the water shone a dull silver as before, and repeated the same endless eddies.

The surrounding fields suddenly looked different. The beautiful moon-soaked night-scene, through which I now had to move with nothing but a bayonet for protection, had grown a hundred times larger. No longer was it knitted together by the protective range of my rifle; instead, it stretched out on all sides, having become, as it were, the infinite accumulation of short radii to which my bayonet would reach.

For a moment I glanced back regretfully at the river. Yet I knew at once that apart from the difficulty of restoring the rifle to use after it had lain buried in the mud of the river bed, I would, even were I to recover it, simply be obliged to throw it away once more.

I started to walk. I hurried along with a slouch between the fields and the moon-permeated mist. Soon I was in the forest. The moonlight was strewn on the path, and the spaces between the trees were filled irregularly with light and shade. The turtledoves were singing two familiar bars of a Beethoven symphony that I recognized from the previous night.

I was lonely. I was terrifyingly lonely. Why did I have to return to the mountains harboring this loneliness? This was the path I had thought last night I would never pass again. That I should be walking along it now in the opposite direction seemed even stranger than had the idea of not seeing it again.

I could visualize my future spread out before me—a future of infinite monotony, circumscribed only by my supply of mountain potatoes. Was such a life really worth living? Perhaps not, I answered myself, but was death really worth dying? There was nothing for it but to keep on. I hurried along briskly, almost on my own momentum, toward my life-giving supply of mountain potatoes.

I crossed field after field, made my way through forests, forded streams; and gradually the hills came nearer.

The trail began to rise through a dense, dark forest. Then I passed a field and entered the final wood. As on the previous morning, the speckles on the barks of the trees stood out clearly: once again it was the light of dawn. I felt as if I were being moved forward mechanically like a puppet.

✌
✌
✌ 21 ✌ *COMPANIONS*

When I emerged from the wood I immediately caught sight in the early morning light of three figures moving about on my potato field. Their service caps and green shirts were unmistakable: they could only be Japanese soldiers. I felt tears suddenly rising to my eyes.

"Hey! Hey!" I shouted, waving my arms and running toward them.

They all turned in my direction, like a group of automatic dolls; then they glanced at each other and once more stared at me.

One of them walked up to me. I was taken aback by his stern expression. From his chevrons I could see that he was a corporal; he was clearly the squad leader.

"What company are you from?" he said.

I remembered that, technically at least, I was still part of a military organization. I saluted formally and answered: "Private First Class Tamura, sir. Koizumi Corps, Murayama Company."

"Murayama Company?" said a young superior-private who now approached us. "I thought they were all wiped out at Albuera." His face was peaked and unshaven, but his eyes, which shone vivaciously under a pair of thick eyebrows, told me that he was still on active service.

"I was in the hospital when the bombing started. I made my way here all alone."

"Oh, it was you, was it?" said the third member of the group, who was, like myself, a first-class private. "I knew someone must have been up here when we found the helmet. Where have you come from now?"

I told them what had happened to me since leaving

the mountains the night before; however, I did not mention having killed the Filipino woman.

"Hm," said the corporal, eyeing me suspiciously. "You've really done some hiking around by yourself, haven't you? Where's your rifle?"

"It got lost in the valley, sir, on my way back last night," I said, automatically blurting out the lie.

"Very efficient of you, wasn't it?" said the corporal. "Of course," he added, looking at the superior-private, "you went and lost yours too, didn't you—at Burauen."

"What the hell!" said the superior-private gruffly. "We were all running for our lives through the middle of that damned forest, remember? It was so dark you couldn't possibly find something once you'd dropped it. Don't worry, though, corporal, I'll pick up another one before long."

"Off some poor dead soldier, eh?" said the corporal, laughing.

"What company are you from, sir?" I said to the squad leader.

"We're from the Oshima Company. We tried to fight our way across to Burauen, but the whole company got cut to pieces. We were meant to join up with a parachute unit. A fat lot of good they did us! They were all shot up before they could even land. Only thirty of

them reached the ground alive. And all they could do was
to scurry into the jungle for safety. Thanks to them, the
Americans just about managed to wipe out our whole
company. Me and my men here got back to the coast,
but we didn't have a bullet or a piece of food left between us. Then suddenly we came on this field and we
could breathe again."

I glanced around and saw that my former paradise
had been utterly laid waste. The "potato trees" had all
been uprooted and there was a large pile of potatoes near
the hut.

"Luckiest thing that ever happened—finding those
spuds," continued the corporal. "They should see us
through as far as Palompon."

Palompon was a town on one tip of the peninsula that
protrudes in the northwest of Leyte Island. I knew that
it had been heavily reinforced by our troops.

"Is your squad heading for Palompon, sir?"

"Didn't you know? The Army's given orders for all
troops on Leyte to muster at Palompon. The General
Staff finally seems to have caught on that the campaign
isn't going quite as they'd planned. In the past week all
the units have been falling back on Palompon. They say
we're going to be evacuated by troopship to Cebu.
Funny you not having heard! That's what comes from

staying on your own—you don't get to hear the orders."

"No, I never heard them."

"All right, men," said the corporal after a pause, "we'll dig up all the spuds we can carry and then we'll clear out. You'd better dig yourself a few," he added to me, "to help you get to Palompon."

"Very well, sir."

The soldiers glanced at each other.

"Makes us feel like a bunch of damned barbarians," said the superior-private, "hearing someone say 'Very well, sir.' I can't remember when I heard that last. Look here, fellow," he added, turning to me, "no one's telling you to come along with us or anything. I shouldn't think you could keep up with us anyhow, seeing as you've been ill."

"I'll do my best to keep up with you," I answered.

"Well, fellow, I'll tell you one thing. The three of us here are a bunch of real hard-bitten old soldiers. We went through the whole New Guinea campaign together —right down to the bitter end when we were living on human flesh. . . . If you really want to come with us, you'd better look sharp or we'll be eating you with our potatoes!"

They all guffawed. Then the superior-private noticed my haversack.

"What's all that stuff you've got in there?" he said. "It's pretty bulky, isn't it?"

"It's salt," I said.

"Salt?" The three men shouted out the word in unison like a paean of joy.

"Salt!" repeated the corporal, his voice suddenly assuming a respectful tone. "You're a real millionaire, you know. Well . . . well, what about it? Aren't you going to let us have a taste? There's no sense hogging it all yourself, is there? We'll take you along to Palompon with us. And don't worry—we won't eat you! That was just a joke."

I could hardly demur.

"All right," I said feebly, "help yourselves."

"Really?" said the superior-private. "That's damned nice of you, fellow! We'll take it over there to the hut and share it out, shall we? But first let's have a quick taste."

They all crammed their hands into my haversack, pulled out fistfuls of salt and stuffed it in their mouths. As they chewed they mumbled their appreciation. I noticed that the eyes of the superior-private were filmed with tears.

"Where on earth did you get it?" he said, as we started toward the hut.

"Down in the village."

"Did you see anything else?"

"No, there was just salt."

"Surely there must have been some other food. Are you sure you looked everywhere?"

"Only in the one house."

"That's too bad, you know, that's really too bad. I bet there's lots of other stuff. . . . What about coming down with me and having another look around?"

"The village is probably full of snipers by now."

"Yes, I suppose you're right. In fact, we shouldn't stick around here too long either."

I looked down toward the village. From the same hill where I had seen the prairie fire the day before rose a slender wisp of smoke. The familiar shape of the cross still gleamed above the distant forest, but now that I had found companions it no longer made any impression on me.

For hope had sprung up within me. What I had seen and done in the village still stuck to the back of my mind like the fragments of some terrible nightmare; but the news about Palompon superseded everything. When I considered how swiftly this scrap of news had lifted me from the nadir of despair to a sanguine belief in my own survival, I realized that all the murky visions and experiences I had suffered since leaving my unit had been simply the results of my solitude.

Now I had companions—companions, who, thanks to my gift of salt, were bound to me in a social relationship, and who could not summarily reject me as my squad leader had done. Even my recent homicide seemed unimportant in the light of this new-found relationship; it was almost as if that murder had never happened. I was now an ordinary Japanese soldier, like the thousands of other routed soldiers on the island, and I had the same claim as they to be evacuated to Cebu and eventually to return home alive.

That I should have become gullible enough to believe that for these routed and demoralized soldiers a few handfuls of salt would constitute a bond of comradeship, was itself, of course, the result of my weeks of isolation.

Feathers were scattered about the hut.

"So you actually managed to shoot those chickens," I said.

"No, we caught a couple and wrung their necks," said the superior-private with a chuckle. "The others all got away."

I distributed my salt to my new companions. As I

handed each man his portion I felt that I was performing a sort of ritual that would link us together. I could not tell whether they shared my impression, but in any case their faces all bore the same look of solemn gratitude.

"Well, men, let's go," said the corporal. "Tamura, you'd better hurry up and pick yourself some spuds. I suppose we ought to let you have some of ours after all that salt you've given us, but we'll be needing all the po-tatoes we can carry." He glanced around the field. "We haven't left you very many, have we?" he said, laughing. "I hope you'll excuse us for making such a mess of your property!"

The corporal was clearly in a good humor.

🗡
🗡

🗡 22 🗡 *THE PROCESSION*

I broke off a few of the remaining stems, dis-carded the interior mechanism of my gas mask, as I had seen my companions do, and stuffed the potatoes into the empty case.

Then we set off. The corporal led us down the path

I had taken when I first came up to my field. We reached the river and followed it downstream for a long way until the path veered off at the foot of a new hill. Now we were heading straight north. From what I gathered, the American forces on the east and west coasts had already joined up, thus cutting off the northern part of the island; but, according to the corporal, there was a junction at which the Ormoc Highway branched off to the west, and if we took this road, we should be able to get through to the peninsula and to Palompon.

We crossed the foothills and made our way along a narrow trail over two mountain passes. Finally we reached flat country and the trail became wide enough for an oxcart.

"Better start looking out for planes," said the corporal. "They always strafe the roads."

Now scattered groups of soldiers began to appear from the forests on the hills and joined the road. Soon we were part of a long, serpentine formation with enough men to make a whole company.

When the road emerged into open country, we broke formation and hurried between the bordering trees until it once more entered the shelter of the woods. As our column passed through the virgin forests they became as bustling and congested as the shopping-quarter of some city.

The condition of the troops had deteriorated unbelievably since I had last seen them. Their uniforms were in shreds, their shoes broken, their hair and beards absurdly long. In the soldiers' pale, dirty faces only their eyes shone clearly as they peered inquiringly at each other.

Palompon, Palompon. With that one magic word in his mind, each soldier dragged his sick, starved, exhausted body along the road, desperately trying not to lag behind the others. On the slopes on both sides were rows of soldiers who had lain down to rest, or who had collapsed and been pushed off the road.

I wondered whether the Americans knew our orders about going to Palompon. As if to answer me, the roar of a plane passed low over the forest through which we were filing. I heard the harsh staccato of machine-gun fire. We all scurried for safety. When the plane had passed, the road was littered with more bodies of the dead and wounded.

Night fell suddenly. The corporal led our group off the road into a clearing in the valley. I copied my companions as they extracted the powder from their cartridges and made a fire by rubbing the powder with branches. I recalled how I had chewed away at my raw potatoes day after day, and how I had terrified the Filipino couple with my demand for a match. It could all have been avoided if only I had thought of this simple expedient. As I started to eat my first hot food in weeks I was astounded at my own stupidity.

In the entire ragged procession, we were undoubtedly the only soldiers with an adequate supply of food. It was for this reason that we took our meals in secret.

When we had finished eating we rejoined the file and advanced steadily through the moonlight. In the darkness under the trees, the bayonets and canteens of the marching soldiers clanged against each other.

As soon as dawn came we left the road and slept under the trees; in the evening we started marching again. It was cooler at night and also there was less danger of being strafed. After some days, however, the moon waned and we had to revert to daytime marches.

The number of bodies by the roadside increased steadily. I was on the lookout for a rifle, but none of the corpses seemed to be armed. Either the men had dropped their rifles some time before their final collapse, or their fellow soldiers had stolen them promptly afterward.

One day the corporal ran up to me with a rifle. "Here, Tamura, I've found one for you," he said and handed it to me.

"Is it a dead man's?" I asked.

He looked at me in astonishment.

"If I didn't pinch it from a stiff," he said, "where the hell d'you think I got the thing? You needn't have it if you don't want it."

"Damned fool!" the superior-private hissed in my ear. "If the squad leader gives you something, you'd damned well better take it without asking a lot of silly questions!" I noticed that he had acquired a rifle of his own since our departure from the potato field.

"Yes, sir," I said to the corporal. "Thank you very much."

Each time I passed a soldier who had collapsed by the roadside I felt a vague oppression in my chest. I remembered how, after the bombing of the hospital, I had been able to laugh and turn my back on my unfortunate companions as they had scurried about absurdly in the valley below. That was because my own death had then seemed so imminent. Now, however, that Palompon had emerged as a symbol of hope, I could not restrain a feeling of guilt towards my fellow soldiers who would never reach this haven.

Yet after some days I began to grow accustomed to them. I saw that they were not just lying at random by the roadside. Most of them were still alive. Some had settled down by tree trunks and lay there quietly, with their belongings arranged neatly beside them. Others sat cross-legged and fixed the passers-by with their glistening, moribund eyes. One soldier lay flat on the grass and intoned monotonously as the procession passed by: "Anyone here from the Yamanaka Company? Anyone here from the Yamanaka Company?"

One day I noticed two familiar soldiers by the side of the road. I recognized them as Yasuda, the middle-aged soldier with ulcers, and his young companion, Nagamatsu. Since I had last seen them outside the hospital, however, their physical conditions had evidently been reversed; for now it was Yasuda who could not walk, while Nagamatsu had become quite agile. The young man was selling tobacco to the passers-by.

"Anyone want some tobacco? The normal price is three potatoes for a leaf," he announced, "but two potatoes will do."

The Army's purchasing power, however, had drastically declined since the days outside the hospital and there seemed to be no offers.

"Tobacco indeed!" said our corporal, as we passed

Nagamatsu. "Who the hell d'you think's going to buy tobacco now, you damned idiot? Of course," he added with a sneer, "you might try selling some to the General Staff. They'll be along here any minute!"

"Are you sure?" said Nagamatsu eagerly. And then he recognized me.

"Good heavens, Tamura!" he said. "Don't tell me you're still alive!"

"Well," I said, "I suppose I am. What's happened to you two?"

Signaling to my companions that I would catch up with them, I stepped out of the procession and joined Nagamatsu.

"It doesn't bear speaking about," he said. "I'm just about done for!"

"How?"

"It's that terrible creature over there!" he said, glancing at Yasuda, who was sitting under a tent by a clump of trees some ten yards from the road.

"Terrible?" I said.

"Well, I'll tell you," said Nagamatsu. "After the hospital was bombed, I decided to tag along with the old geezer. That was all right, but it didn't take me long to find out he had to have every single thing his own way. He's made me his servant in everything but name. Now he's got me selling this tobacco here. The old geezer can't move an inch by himself."

I looked at Yasuda. He was leaning against a tree with his right leg stretched out helplessly in front of him. I walked over to the tent.

"My, my," he said when he saw me. "So it's Tamura, is it? You're looking a bit fatter, you know. Been getting plenty to eat, have you?"

"I'm not quite sure how," I said, "but I seem to have managed somehow."

"Well, I've managed up till now too," said Yasuda, "thanks to young Nagamatsu here. But I'm not so sure about the future."

"I don't suppose any of us are," I said. "That leg of yours must make it difficult."

"Nagamatsu lets me lean on his shoulder and I drag myself along somehow or other."

"His shoulder?" I said, amazed that in this routed remnant of an army there should still be room for such altruism.

"I don't have all that much choice," said Nagamatsu with a wry smile. "If I didn't let him lean on my shoulder, I wouldn't eat. I ran out of food ages ago, you see. Since then I've been living off Yasuda's tobacco."

"That's right," said Yasuda. "We've got to reach

Palompon before my tobacco runs out, or we're done for!"

"The trouble is," said Nagamatsu, "it's not so easy to get rid of the stuff any longer."

"Nonsense!" said Yasuda. "However bad things get, people still need tobacco. "It's funny, you know, Tamura, but that's the one thing they can't do without. We don't sell much at a time, of course, but still there's a steady demand."

"But there isn't, Dad," said Nagamatsu.

"How d'you mean there isn't?" said Yasuda indignantly. "It's only because you're such a rotten salesman. I've told you a dozen times—soldiers will sell their last spud for a pinch of tobacco!"

As we talked the procession passed uninterruptedly along the road. Presently a group of officers appeared. When he saw them, Nagamatsu dashed forward, saluted and held out a tobacco leaf. One of the officers nodded and took the leaf. An N.C.O., who was walking next to the officer, ran up to Nagamatsu and struck him across the cheek.

"Silly idiot!" he screamed. "Trading tobacco at a time like this! You'd damned well better get back into line and keep heading for Palompon, or you'll be sorry! D'you hear?"

Then the group moved along the road and disappeared around a corner.

Nagamatsu walked back to the tent, rubbing his cheek. Now it was Yasuda's turn to storm at him.

"You stupid fool!" he shouted. "What the hell d'you mean handing over the goods before getting anything in exchange? When are you going to stop acting like a damned half-wit?"

"But Dad, it's the first time that's happened to me," said Nagamatsu ruefully.

"Well, look out or it'll happen again—you poor moron. . . ."

As Yasuda continued his abuse, I decided that it was time for me to leave. I said good-by and started toward the road. Yasuda glared at me, his eyes still full of anger, but Nagamatsu followed me, as if to postpone the moment of parting.

"I've just about had all I can take from that creature," he muttered.

"Well," I said, "if you've had enough, I suggest you leave him and strike out on your own. I certainly don't see why you should stick by someone who speaks to you the way he does."

"I know," he said. "The trouble is, I don't think I can

manage by myself. Without his tobacco, I'd starve—that's the long and short of it!"

"If tobacco's all that important, why don't you just help yourself to some and clear out?"

"That's no good either," said Nagamatsu. "He won't let the stuff out of his sight. Each time there's some business, he doles out exactly one leaf."

I could not help laughing when I realized how neatly Yasuda had trapped the weak-minded young soldier.

"I still think you'd be better off making your way to Palompon," I said, "than wasting your time around here trying to trade tobacco."

"The fact is," said Nagamatsu, lowering his voice, "Yasuda doesn't figure on going to Palompon. The first American he meets, he's going to stick his hands up. The trouble is, though, the only time we ever get near any Americans, they're in planes or firing trench mortars. Even Yasuda can't get very far with them!"

I gazed into Nagamatsu's pale face.

"Are you planning to surrender also?" I asked.

"I really won't know till the time comes," he said, looking down. "But I expect I'll do whatever Yasuda does."

We had reached the road now. I said good-by to

Nagamatsu and set off in pursuit of my companions. Yet however fast I walked, I did not seem able to catch up with them.

🦋
🦋
🦋   23   🦋   *THE RAIN*

All day long a moist, heavy wind blew through the forest with the body temperature of a living creature. Then the rain began. It swished down through the branches onto the heads of the marching soldiers. The rainy season had come to Leyte.

The water gradually accumulated on the volcanic gravel that filled the spaces between the grass on the road. In level country it made a pleasant squelching sound under our boots; but on the slippery red clay of the slopes the going became harder and harder for the troops, worn out, as most of us already were, by undernourishment and beriberi.

The rain beat down mechanically like a shower bath. Sometimes it would stop abruptly only to start again in a few minutes, as if a tap had been turned on. So it continued day in, day out.

Before long we were all wet to the skin. Our sodden haversacks seemed several times their normal weight and the cords cut painfully into our shoulders. The narrow straps of the steel helmets, which we carried on our backs, began to chafe: soon the roadside was dotted with abandoned helmets.

I quickened my pace in a desperate effort to overtake the corporal and his two men, but although they could not have been very far ahead of me, I no longer had sufficient strength to make up for the time I had lost by the roadside. After two days of useless exertion I resigned myself to abandoning the good will of my companions into which I had so hopefully invested my salt.

The water had begun to flow in rapid rivulets over the grass by the roadside. Some of the soldiers in the last stages of exhaustion tried to revive themselves by dipping their bodies in the water. A few lay completely inert with their faces immersed and looked as if they had stopped breathing. As we passed one such lifeless figure the soldier next to me said: "Poor bastard! That's how we'll all end up." To my amazement, the "corpse" lifted up its face, all dripping with water, and murmured: "What's that you say?" We hurried on.

Many of the bodies had begun to swell like the ones that I had seen in the seaside village: these, I knew, were really dead. Maggots drifted on the surface of the water, and, gathering in clumps of grass a few feet from the corpses, floated there in wriggling masses.

The corpses were devoid of everything but the sodden uniforms that were stretched tightly over their bloated bodies. Their shoes had been removed and their bare feet, bleached by the water, were swollen like the feet of the angels in the primitive Buddhist paintings of the Hakuchō Period.

Mixed with the sour vegetable smell of the rain-soaked grass, that pungent odor which I knew so well began to hover over the greenery.

On the rare occasions when it stopped raining, a dazzling sun would thrust its way through the branches of the trees. Then we would strip and spread our clothes out to dry. Our bodies were filthy and emaciated; but to my eyes there was something strangely impressive about these scenes, in which on the steaming green undergrowth the brown color of the soldiers' naked limbs mixed with the greenish yellow of their uniforms and the white of their underclothes.

Thanks to the rain, American planes had grown scarce; but in their place our procession was constantly harassed from the flank by well-armed Filipino guerrillas. The path that we had so far taken followed the foothills to the west of the central mountain range. The guerrilla attacks, however, forced us to strike inland and to make our way northward, parallel to the coast, along the narrow mountain trails. Often when we crossed the mountain streams, which had swollen now into huge muddy rapids, the starved and battered soldiers would be swept off their feet by the swirling waters and carried helplessly downstream.

After we had passed the lights of Ormoc to our left, the mountains of the central range became lower, and we could see the hills and valleys following each other in rapid succession. Our path ran along the backs of the low hills that rolled along the seashore; their summits looked in outline like great waves as they curled back after breaking on the beach. The level country between these hills and the foothills of the central range was covered with mud, as if it had been under a flood.

All around us the hills and fields were reeking in the tropical rain. Occasionally clouds would drift down and drape the trees on the hilltops, only to be puffed away by sudden gusts of wind. As the rain swept down in wide sheets over the fields it seemed to be striped with moving lines.

Now the pace of our drenched procession became slower and the distance between the individual soldiers

greater. Their soggy shoes and rubber-soled socks split
and were left by the roadside. The criterion of un-
usability seemed to vary from soldier to soldier: some
of the less exigent men would pick up shoes that others
had abandoned and wear them until they found another
pair, and thus would continue on their way, constantly
changing shoes.

The shoes I had been wearing since I left my unit
had already been cracked in the soles when I had come
down from the potato field. One day they both split
neatly in two from tip to toe. From then on I went
barefoot.

24 *THREE-FORK JUNCTION*

The peninsula for which we were all aiming
sticks out like a great ear to the northwest of Leyte. A
low range of mountains stretches down from the north
of the peninsula and envelops the bay in the south. In the
farthest inlet of the bay—in the root of the ear, so to

speak—lies the town of Ormoc, which was originally
our base.

The mountains on the peninsula run parallel to the
main mountain range of the island, though evidently
belonging to a different system. Between the two ranges
were enormous stretches of low-lying marshes. Here the
so-called Ormoc Highway ran from Ormoc in the south
to Carigara on the north coast, then around the northern
foothills of the central range and down through the
great plains to Tacloban on the east coast. With their
east-west link-up, the Americans had captured Limon,
Valencia, and all the other strategic points on the Ormoc
Highway. Their tanks and trucks ran ceaselessly along
the great road, which was protected at regular intervals
by guerrilla posts. If we were to enter the peninsula and
reach the town of Palompon on its southwestern extremity, we would somehow have to break through this road.
The vital point on our retreat was a place known as
Three-Fork Junction, which lay north of Limon on the
Ormoc Highway, and from where a road branched off
to the left for the peninsula. If only we could make our
way safely to this road, we should—or so at least we
imagined—have an easy march as far as Palompon.

As we neared the highway we passed one of our
picked units, which earlier in the campaign had suc-

ceeded for a while in delaying the American advance from the east coast, and which even now preserved a modicum of tactical organization. That night we could hear the familiar crackle of Japanese machine guns and small-arms fire, as the picked unit tried to make a breach in the road.

"Damn it all!" muttered an N.C.O. who lay near me. "Why do they have to put on a show like that just when we're trying to slip across the highway? Now we'll never get past. The Americans will be on the lookout."

The field in which we were camped was surrounded by hills on three sides, and the hill straight in front of us was like the bottom of a deep purse. The next day I decided to go up and see what lay ahead. I clambered to the top, where a group of soldiers was gathered, hid behind a bush, and scanned the scene.

About a hundred yards ahead across the marshes a single wide streak of road, supported by an embankment, cut its way across my field of vision; this was the Ormoc Highway.

On the left across the road, the marshland stretched into the distance until it reached a forest. Here and there in the marsh the silhouette of a huge, solitary acacia tree emerged hazily like an island. To the right, a thickly wooded hill jutted forth, and all around its base low-lying thickets were spread across the marsh like the trains of a skirt.

Beyond the forest on the left, rose a rocky, cloud-swathed mountain. This was Kanquipot, the main peak of the peninsular mountain range. The Japanese soldiers had rechristened it *Kanki-Hō,* or the Peak of Joy, but, as it turned out, it would more appropriately have been called the Peak of Terror.

At the far right-hand extremity of the highway, a cluster of houses indicated Three-Fork Junction. I could see the road for Palompon branching off to the left, entering the forest, and circling the base of the foothills as it headed toward Kanquipot.

"If we can just get as far as that forest, we'll be all right," said one of the soldiers on the hill.

Now and then American trucks and green jeeps crawled along the highway. This was the first time that I had seen the "enemy" so close at hand. Soldiers with heavy steel helmets stood in the trucks and from time to time fired their automatic rifles at random in the direction of our hill. Occasionally they shouted something I could not make out.

"Damn their hides!" muttered someone nearby. "They're as fat as pigs, aren't they? I bet those bastards never have to go short of anything!"

I could not see who was talking, because he was hidden behind some trees, but I recognized the harse tone of voice: it was the corporal whom I had some days before given up all hope of overtaking.

"Aren't you the squad leader I was with, sir?" I exclaimed automatically and scrambled to my feet.

"Don't talk so loud, damn it!" said an N.C.O. who was squatting nearby.

I walked between the trees and found my companions —the first-class private, the superior-private, and, sprawling on the ground with his gaiters removed, the corporal. He did not appear to be too pleased to see me.

"What, are you still around?" he said.

"Yes, I got held up talking to my friends. I'm very sorry, sir."

"Nothing to be sorry about," he said with a sardonic smile. "Anyhow, you've come just in time to join us for a delightful little expedition across that road."

"Will we be crossing it tonight, sir?"

"That's right, we're waiting till it gets dark. But it's going to be tough going through those marshes, I can tell you."

I gazed across the hundred yards or so of mud that separated our hill from the highway. The terrain was quite different from any that I had tackled until now.

On the surface of the water floated green clumps that looked like waterweed.

The superior-private was also scanning the marsh.

"I wonder how deep it is," he said absently.

"There's no telling from up here," said the corporal, "but it's pretty damned deep. I'd have thought there was some better place to cross the road than through that filthy bog. But everyone else seems to be assembling here, so I suppose this is the best place."

"From here to the road the mud's up to one's knees," said a soldier who was lying at a small distance from our group, "but the other side isn't supposed to be too bad."

"Fine, fine," said the corporal, "you're a real mine of information, aren't you? I suppose you've been across that marsh plenty of times yourself."

Even here on the front, where extreme skepticism was the order of the day, I was struck by the sarcasm of the corporal's tone. The man who had spoken was silent for a while, and I wondered whether he had been offended; finally he muttered: "I heard it from a fellow who used to be in the supply dump at Three-Fork Junction. But if you don't believe it, I really don't give a damn! You can just go to hell!"

So saying, he stood up and walked away. He was a

tall, loose-limbed man and he moved unsteadily along the hilltop.

"Well, he's a queer customer, isn't he?" said the corporal, with the same smile fixed on his face. "What did he have to get into such a huff about?"

"Hell, what difference does it make?" said the superior-private. "The only thing that matters now is to get through to Palompon." Then, with the deep-rooted cynicism of the foot soldier, he added: "Yes, we'd better get there in time to wave good-by to the General Staff as they set sail for Cebu and leave us to hold the fort!"

The first-class private, who had impressed me as the least tough of my companions, came up to me.

"Hey, Tamura, have you still got any of that salt left?"

The salt in my haversack had been thoroughly saturated by the rain. I had run out of potatoes some time before, and for several days now my only subsistence had been the brine that oozed through my haversack.

"Yes, I do, but . . ."

"I don't, you know. The squad leader confiscated all of mine. Come on, be a good fellow and let me have some, won't you?"

Reluctantly I opened my haversack. The dark, rough, rain-soaked Philippine salt had hardened into a sort of cake together with the dirt at the bottom of the bag. I was about to extract a piece when the first-class private stopped me.

"Wait a minute," he said. "Let's go over there."

I followed him to another part of the hill, out of eyeshot of the corporal, and handed him a gray hunk of salt. He thanked me profusely and gulped it down.

"Look here, Tamura," he said. "I'm going to give you a good tip."

I waited in silence.

"You shouldn't tag along with us the way you do, saying 'Yes, sir,' 'No, sir,' 'Thank you, sir' every few minutes to the squad leader. I've been with the corporal ever since we landed on New Guinea and I wouldn't treat a dog the way he's treated us. He's never done one single thing for his men. He wasn't so bad when we were stationed at headquarters, but as soon as we got to the front, he became a real bastard. Just because he thinks he knows something about fighting, he feels he can treat us all like dirt. He'll do the same thing to you. If you keep tagging along like this, he'll clean you out of all your salt and in the bargain he'll probably . . . he'll probably get rid of you."

"Tell me," I said, "were you fellows joking when you talked about eating human flesh in New Guinea?"

"Human flesh?" he said and, turning his eyes dreamily to the sky, remained silent for a few moments.

"Yes," he said, "you'd better take it that we were joking. But listen here, I'll tell you something a lot more interesting than that. It happened just when we were being cleared out of Buna. It was a tougher march than this one, I can tell you. One day we found a young soldier who'd been shot through the chest. He'd crawled as far as the roadside and was lying there more dead than alive. When we reached him, he said: 'Kill that fellow! He's a traitor! Kill him!' Well, we had no idea who 'that fellow' was, but finally we managed to piece his story together and found out it was his squad leader. The two of them had been retreating together through the island, you see. The squad leader had decided to surrender and was trying to talk the young fellow into doing the same thing. But he wouldn't listen to him, you see, so that squad leader just shot him in cold blood and walked on by himself. Some bastard, eh? I don't see why he had to go and shoot him, do you?—just because he wouldn't surrender."

"No."

"We had a fine bunch of men then. But there were

some real swine among the squad leaders, I can tell
you! So . . ."

"Yes?"

"So—well, I'm not saying our own squad leader is
quite that bad, but still I don't know what the hell goes
on inside any of them—squad leaders, N.C.O.'s, officers,
and all. I'm stuck in the ranks with my unit, so there's
nothing I can do about it. But you're free to come and
go as you like, aren't you? I suppose it gets pretty lone-
some being all by yourself in a place like this. Still, if
you ask me, you'll be better off if you stay that way."

"I see."

"Are you sure you see?" he said as we started walking
back to our original position. "Well, don't forget what
I've told you. And stop tagging along like you have."

The corporal looked askance at us as we approached.

"What have you two been conspiring about?" he
said. "Planning how to surrender, eh? Well, this is your
big chance. Once we get to Palompon, you won't be
seeing any more Americans. . . . Look, there are some
more of them passing now. Aren't they charming!"

Down on the highway, a jeep moved past, with
TRAVELING CHAPLAIN painted on the side. A small, elderly man in a khaki uniform was leaning out of the

window and nervously glancing at both sides of the road.

"Hey, you!" barked the corporal's voice. I turned around and found the muzzle of his rifle pointing straight at me.

"If you think you can surrender, just try doing it!" he said. "You really figure you can get away with it, do you, you shameless bastard? Well, you can't! You tried dropping out of ranks once before, but now I'm going to see that you get to Palompon if I have to drag you every inch of the way myself. So you'd better make up your mind to it! And you needn't make such a face about it either!" he added, laughing merrily to himself.

🚩
🚩
🚩 25 🚩 *THE FLASHES OF LIGHT*

The rain still pelted down, clouding the swamp, and gradually the dusk gathered. First the distant peak of Kanquipot disappeared, then the acacia trees and the forest ahead; before long it was pitch dark. The traffic along the Ormoc Highway came to a standstill.

As if this was the long-awaited moment, a sound arose in the darkness—a sound of heavy bodies slipping down the wet slope amidst excited whispering.

I had a feeling that the corporal also had started down the hill.

"Are we to cross the road now, sir?" I asked.

"Don't talk, you blasted idiot!" hissed someone from nearby. "Say another word and I'll brain you!"

I slid down the slope feet first, bumping into a tree on the way and getting caught in a clump of bushes. The sound continued on both sides, but when I reached the bottom, it stopped. I could not tell whether there was anyone else at the foot of the hill, nor could I try to find the corporal.

In the marsh ahead there was not a sign of anything moving. For a moment the terrible thought struck me that the breakthrough might have been called off due to some last-minute hitch and that I was down there by myself. Then there was a noise in the darkness in front of me. It sounded like a mess tin clanging against a bayonet. As if called into action by the noise, my feet started to move forward.

As I stepped over a clump of thick grass I could hear the sound of running water. The next moment my bare foot touched the water and my leg began to sink in. The following step brought me onto another clump of grass. Then I sank in more than two feet and the mud started in earnest.

At each step I was up to my knees in the thick slime. The soles of my feet slipped far down, without feeling the slightest solid foundation. I had the uncomfortable sensation of being supported only by the thickness of the mud that I had myself pressed down. The mud became deeper and deeper as I advanced, and the weight of my rifle seemed to push me down still farther.

Opaque darkness spread out on all sides. The rain had stopped and the only sound was the intermittent howling of a dog, which was wafted from the distance through the muggy atmosphere.

Now and then I glanced up and could make out the line of the embankment cutting its way sharply through the darkness ahead of me; it appeared to border directly on the black sky. Yet each time I looked it seemed to be just as far away.

The mud, which had become still deeper, now was above my knees. I drew one leg high out of the bog and, balancing myself on the other leg, which sank steadily into the ground, described a great arc with my free leg, as if to sweep the surface of the mud, and thrust it forward. Then, transferring all my weight to the leg that in its turn began to glide down with a slushy sound, I pulled out my other leg from behind and forced it ahead.

Soon I was utterly exhausted. I knew that if the mud ahead became any deeper, I should not be able to move forward at all. Dawn would find me here, with the upper half of my body emerging from the ground: I should be literally a stick-in-the-mud, ready to be potted by the first American soldier who passed along the highway.

It was a petrifying moment. I wondered whether the other soldiers also were sinking into this terrible mud. Could they all be in my predicament? I was desperately anxious to make sure, but my recent upbraiding prevented me from calling to my fellow soldiers.

I thought of going back; but to walk through the mud that I had already passed seemed no less impossible than advancing. There was nothing for it: I must plow my way ahead as far as I could, and if the time came when I could no longer advance—well, I should simply be killed. That, after all, was the very worst that could happen to me—and how many times in the past weeks had I not calmly resigned myself to just that fate?

Now the notion of death gave me a sense of comfort, as if I had been told that I was to return home. Here at least was something on which I could always rely, something certain that would wait for me patiently at my destination, wherever I went and whatever I tried to do.

Suddenly my heart felt light and new strength seemed to bubble through my body. The action of forcing one leg after another out of the mud was now no longer a painful compulsion, but simple and voluntary. At the same time I had the impression that I was advancing rapidly.

Accompanying this new sense of ease I had the strange feeling that my movements were being observed by someone. I stood still. No, of course not—how could anyone be watching me here in this dark, silent muddiness? I started to walk ahead, but realized almost at once that I had in fact been observed. Proof was that no sooner had I rejected the feeling that I was being seen than my actions lost their free, voluntary quality and also their rapidity.

All of a sudden the embankment confronted me. Now I could hear the sound of men breathing. I stretched out my hand and touched the scabbard of the man ahead of me. Instinctively I grasped it. "Let go, damn you, let go!" he muttered under his breath. I thought that I recognized the corporal's voice.

The mud gradually became shallower; then I was in it again up to my thighs, and a moment later I stepped on to a hard shelf of earth. I was on the bottom of the embankment. I lowered my rifle.

As I scrambled about six feet up along the grass slope of the embankment I could sense human forms moving all round me. There was a rustling sound as we crawled up clinging to the roots of the grass.

In the darkness the white surface of the highway stretched from left to right. I crawled across it, with my elbow touching the gravel and my rifle trailing behind. The whiteness was dotted with the black antlike figures of the other men. Once again the barking of a dog reached me.

I rapidly slid down the grass slope on the opposite side of the road. I heard the noise of running water and began to walk away from the road. Here the mud covered only my ankles; the information of the tall soldier on the hilltop had evidently been correct. I had been walking in a crouching position, but now I inadvertently straightened myself up.

"Get down on your belly and crawl, you idiot!" whispered a voice.

I crawled ahead rapidly on my hands and knees. In front of us was the dark outline of the forest through which passed the road to Palompon. If we could just reach that forest, everything would be all right.

The surrounding darkness crawled ahead with me—a darkness that I felt was full of my fellow soldiers. I realized that once again I had stopped being "I" and become part of a collective "we."

Ping!

The sound of metal striking metal broke into our crawling group. A light came from ahead and at the same instant, a shower of bullets.

"Tanks!" shouted several voices.

I threw myself flat on my stomach and glanced up. In the forest ahead a series of lights was lined up like Cyclopean eyes, and as their gleaming shafts crisscrossed over the field where we lay I could make out the prostrate bodies of countless Japanese soldiers.

I pressed my forehead to the ground. Each time a light flashed in the small field of vision on both sides of my head I could feel a gust of air as a bullet tore past directly above me. I began to fall back inch by inch toward the road. Between the rattle of the machine guns, which sounded like someone banging metal, and the thud of the wet ground being kicked high into the air by the bullets, I was vaguely aware (as if I were watching some sort of fast-motion picture) of my own hands and feet moving forward.

"They've got me!" came a voice from the left. Then

on my other side I saw a figure standing up, moving forward with a drawn-out cry of "Oh-h-h," and silently collapsing in the mud. Once again I thought that it was the corporal.

I also stood up and began running. The grass of the embankment was so bright that I felt sure I could see my shadow reflected on it. I ran straight for this brightness. I seemed to remember having seen a ditch at the bottom of the enbankment. If I could get that far . . .

I reached the emerald embankment and tumbled sideways into the ditch. Below me the water bubbled along, while above the bullets whizzed past and the lights from the tanks lit up the side of the embankment. The chances were that I could stay safely in this ditch: it seemed unlikely that the Americans would bring their tanks across the marsh, or that they would carry out a charge.

Eventually the sound of firing stopped and only the searchlights continued to move back and forth, back and forth, along the embankment. Then they went out —all but one light, which remained fixed on the same place like a protracted screech.

In the end it too went out, and once more everything was pitch black and silent. Nothing moved. What could have happened to all the soliers who had crawled with me toward the forest? I had no idea. The darkness that blanketed my eyes, the water which flowed along my body and seemed to have soaked its way through to my skin, the smell of mud and grass—these had become my universe. . . .

I sighed deeply and crawled out of the ditch. The forest lay ahead of me, black and quiet as ever; one might almost have wondered whether the recent carnage had really happened. Again I heard a dog barking.

Now a new sound advanced from the side of the road. It was rain. With it came a whispering voice; then the sound of some indistinct song and a noise as of someone tapping tin plate.

I slowly climbed the embankment and after listening carefully for approaching footsteps, scurried across the highway like a toad and rolled head over heels down the opposite slope.

I rested for a while at the bottom before starting out once more across the deep mud. At some time or other I seemed to have lost my rifle and, perhaps because of this, my return journey was less arduous.

🦋
🦋

🦋 26 🦋 *THE APPARITION*

From the cluster of trees on top of the hill I gazed at the road gradually growing white in the dawn. On the other side, between the road and the forest, I could make out the corpses of Japanese soldiers dotted about the fields, but there seemed to be far fewer men than I had seen on the previous night by the light of the tanks. I wondered how many soldiers had managed to get away like me.

The rain stopped. Far away to the west, presumably in the direction of the sea, the sky was thickly heaped with gray clouds; above them rose a huge red cumulus, like a shock of hair.

Kanquipot also was dyed by the rising sun. One part of the mountain, shaped like a man and lit bright red, projected above the purple shadows of the main rocks; it stood out in contrast with the fields and hills below, which were still steeped in the pale light of dawn. That is where most of the other soldiers must have fled. I imagined them now with a sort of nostalgia, as one might recall an old friend with whom one has spent pleasant hours in one's garden at home. At this moment, they were probably waking up by the foot of that mountain and about to start on the wretched rites of preparing themselves for the coming day. There would be no point in my trying to join them. . . .

Then the shooting started. The dry sound of trench mortars arose in the forest ahead and the hill where I lay was riddled with bullets. I scampered down the opposite slope and hid in a hollow, with my back to the line of fire. The range was gradually extended in my direction and soon the roar of explosions surrounded my hollow. Great clouds of dust moved steadily across the plain below and began to crawl up the opposite hill. The air was full of flying tree branches.

The Japanese soldiers had evidently all been scared away by the attack on the previous night, and there was not a single man to be seen. Yet the firing continued relentlessly across the deserted green of the hills and fields.

At one moment the thousands of crisscrossing bullets completely blotted out my field of vision. Then the range of fire moved away toward the central mountain range in the distance.

After about an hour, the artillery fire finally stopped. Then a single airplane skimmed low over the tops of the hills and strafed the forests on the slopes. For a while it disappeared and its distant whirring made a dull echo in the sky; then it roared back over a near-by hill with an earsplitting screech. It zoomed high into the sky with its guns blazing away. After it had attacked the area from every angle, it finally left.

Now all was quiet. I returned to the hill from where I could overlook the great marsh and Three-Fork Junction. The American trucks had started running again on Ormoc Highway. Before they appeared from the left, I could hear the sound of firing in the forest beyond the marsh. The soldiers in the trucks were shooting assiduously in all directions. As they passed below me they would give a loud shout and direct a rain of fire into the trees on the hill where I was lying.

Presently a truck marked with a red cross stopped by the side of the road and a group of medical corps men stepped out. They walked about nonchalantly inspecting the corpses of the Japanese soldiers scattered by the edge of the forest. Then two of them returned to the truck, opened the back doors, and pulled out a heap of stretchers, which they carried back to where the bodies were lying. With practiced movements they spread the stretchers out in a row on the ground. At a word of command they began to load the bodies onto the stretchers; then they carried the stretchers back to the truck and piled them in. One stretcher remained for a while by the roadside. I watched as an American soldier walked up to it and thrust a small white object at the mouth of the body that lay there. A lighter flashed. It was a cigarette. The body was alive!

When all the stretchers had been piled in, the back doors were closed, the Americans jumped in, and the truck drove off.

I held my breath and continued staring at the highway. So that fellow soldier of mine was still alive! He was wounded, but he was alive. Now he would be taken to an American Army hospital, and before long he would be sent back to Japan, where he could walk on crutches over his native soil for many long years, until finally he died a peaceful death from some natural cause. . . . Perhaps, after all, I had not been so lucky the night before when I had escaped to this hill without a scratch.

All day long I gazed at the road, hoping for another Red Cross truck. Traffic continued to pass and the soldiers still fired their warning shots in all directions; but the truck for which I waited did not come.

I do not know whether I had already made up my mind to surrender. I just sat there, vaguely waiting for the Red Cross truck. Logically this had nothing to do with my discovery that the Americans were in the habit of rescuing wounded soldiers; for I myself was not wounded. All I can say is that now, when my hope of escaping alive from Palompon had been frustrated (and the terrifying corporal had disappeared), I was beginning to prepare for surrender.

After a day of fretful waiting and a night spent in thought, my preparedness had turned to sanguine determination. The next problem was how to convey my intention to the "enemy." In the end I settled on the classical method of the white flag. Unfortunately I possessed nothing white but my underpants, and even these were far from sparkling. I could only hope that from a distance they would be recognized as representing a flag of surrender.

An even greater obstacle was the hundred yards of mud that separated me from the highway. If I tried to walk across, waving my ambiguous underpants, I might easily be shot long before I reached the road. The marsh seemed wider in the south, and so the next day at dawn I made my way north along the hills. However, after several hours of walking, the marsh seemed as wide as ever. It began to rain and the mud threatened to become deeper still.

My main fear was that I might run into a Japanese

soldier who would prevent me from carrying out the only remaining course of action that spelled survival. In my state of mind I felt quite capable of killing the first such soldier I met. As luck had it, however, I met no one. When I had walked as far north as Three-Fork Junction, I cut across the deserted settlement and found a point that struck me as suitable for my purpose. It was a thicket about twenty yards from the highway and the mud that I would have to cross did not look too deep.

It was still raining as the sun began to set. Everything seemed to come close—the marsh, the white road, the tree-covered hill. The whole scene struck me as resembling the backdrop in a theater. I was no longer in the fields and mountains of the tropics, nor on the battle-front, but in a place where I was to perform a voluntary action—an action whose outcome was undetermined.

"So this is all there is to it!" I thought to myself.

I felt like an actor as I stood there waiting for my cue to enter that voluntarily chosen stage. Then once again I was struck by the feeling that I was being observed by someone.

A jeep appeared along the road and stopped before the thicket where I was hiding; it had evidently had a puncture. Two men jumped out. One went to the back and from where he stood, carefully examined the scene. Once again I was confronted with a great obstacle: that soldier would shoot the moment he caught sight of me.

From the back of the jeep a Filipino woman stepped out, shouting something to the soldiers in a laughing tone. She wore a green American Army uniform and Army gaiters; an automatic rifle rested lightly on her shoulder and a cartridge belt was fastened round her waist. She cut a very gallant figure. I could see her white teeth as she walked up to the soldier who was standing guard and laughed again in her carefree way.

This woman-guerrilla reminded me of my victim in the seaside village. It was then that I knew I could not emerge from my thicket; it was then that I remembered who I was. I was the man who had killed an innocent person! Because I had by chance met some fellow soldiers, I had conceived the hope of returning home alive; later in the course of events I had settled on surrender as a means of survival. Yet this fact remained: even if I should contrive to save my skin, I had forfeited all right to live with my fellow men.

All voluntary actions were forbidden to me. I, who had voluntarily robbed one human life of the compul-

sion whereby it lives, had condemned myself to an existence based entirely on *compulsion*—the compulsion of
moving ineluctably toward my death.

I had already fastened my underpants to a stick. Now
I resignedly laid this "white flag" on the ground. It
occurred to me that I might at once fulfill my final compulsion by emerging from the thicket and exposing myself before the rifle of this woman-guerrilla, who so
closely resembled her whom I had killed.

Just then, from another thicket about twenty yards
down the road, I heard a drawn-out shout of "I surrender!"

A Japanese soldier leaped forth with both hands
raised high above his head and ran onto the highway,
again shouting: "I surrender!"

Once more I had the momentary impression that it
was the corporal. The soldier went on shouting his
declaration of defeat as he ran toward the jeep; then
his feet slipped on the mud and he stumbled.

There was the crack of a rifle, followed by several
more shots as the woman continued firing relentlessly
from the rifle that she held to her hips. The American
soldier excitedly grasped the barrel of the rifle and
tried to wrest it from her while she screamed and strug-
gled with her white teeth bared.

The Japanese soldier lay motionless in the mud. On the back of his green shirt appeared a red spot like a birthmark; gradually it spread over the fabric of the shirt.

A pain ripped through my body, as though it were I who had been shot. Simultaneously a strange thought occurred to me: that it was this Filipino woman who had been observing me two nights before as I stumbled through the mud uncannily aware that a pair of eyes were on me.

🖾
🖾
🖾 27 🖾 *THE FLAME*

Like some benighted traveler of old who gropes his way along a murky path till finally he comes upon a gate, but on knocking receives no reply; and who, finding the gate securely fastened, turns back with his strength exhausted—so I walked away from where the American soldier and the Filipino woman were standing. As I did so, I felt that this was to be the last of that experience of "turning back" which I had repeated so many times since leaving my company.

The surroundings had been ravaged by the previous night's bombardment. The fields were pitted with con-ical holes like those made by ant lions; in the forest, great trees had been felled at their trunks and branches were scattered all about.

Everywhere I saw bodies. Their vivid guts and blood shone in the sun's rain-washed beams, while on the grass their severed legs and arms looked like the remains of so many broken dolls. Only the flies were moving.

At this point begins the period that I have the greatest difficulty in recalling. Although I can confirm from the calendar how many days I must have spent wandering about by myself after the bombardment, I find it remark-ably hard to remember what I did during that period and what I was thinking.

To be sure, it is never possible for us to remember the past exhaustively. Apart from the gaps formed by habit, later experiences often resemble previous ones so closely as to blot them out. As one experience piles up on another, we unconsciously draw strange analogies between the past and the present. It is such accumula-tions of experience that I can remember from that period.

I was certainly living. But I had no consciousness of being alive.

Now that it had become abundantly clear to me, with

the apparition of the Filipino woman whom I had murdered, that I could no longer—whatever luck might come my way—return to the world of human beings, I continued living simply because I was not dead. I no longer had any misgivings; nor did I feel any hatred for the woman by whose death I was condemned.

Even hunger presented no problems. People can eat almost anything. No weed was too tough, no herb too bitter for my palate, so long as I could first make sure, from the fact of insects having nibbled at it, that it was not poisonous.

The rain pelted down, and after I had spent the night under the trees the exposed parts of my body were covered with leeches that had been carried by the water. These delightful, flat-headed, emerald worms, who sucked my blood as I slept, were forthwith added to my menu.

I was walking east toward the central mountain range and at approximately right angles to the Ormoc Highway. Here the valleys twisted their labyrinthine course through a maze of precipitous hills: I judged that in some prehistoric age the area must have been submerged by the sea and subsequently had risen again.

After I had passed monotonous successions of rivers and plains and grass and trees, nature stopped showing the marks of bombardment and I no longer saw the blood-spattered, intestine-wreathed corpses. Instead the air became redolent with a familiar smell: on the road and by the edge of the forests I now began to see the bodies of men who had not died violent deaths.

Some lay on the road with their heads pointing in the direction in which they had been walking; others had crawled to have a drink of water in the ditch that bordered the road and lay there with their heads submerged; others had breathed their last leaning against a tree; still others had been shoved about haphazardly by the force of the wind and the rain that had worked on their bodies since they had died. Some had preserved the emaciated forms in which death had found them, while others had become monstrously swollen, like those I had seen in the seaside village, or again had decomposed still further into liquid and vapor, leaving only a pile of clothed bones to announce the fact of their previous existence. It was strange to look at the uniforms that wrapped these transformed bodies and to see how successfully they had survived their former owners.

One dried-up corpse boasted a fairly decent pair of shoes. I removed them and put them on. Their terrible smell sank into my feet and hands.

I also met living people. One day I saw a barefoot

soldier coming in the opposite direction. He carried only his canteen; like me, he had neither helmet nor rifle.

"Is this the way to Palompon?" he said, panting out the words.

"I expect so. But the Americans are there and you'll never get through."

He sat down limply, as if deflated by my answer; I could see that he was dead tired. I looked him over carefully to make sure that he had nothing which I might need, then continued on my way.

The fields and hills were hazed by the rain. With the wind came the rustling of trees, and from the side the rain gradually drew an opaque curtain over the scene.

At night it continued to pour in torrents. I chose a thick clump of leaves for my bed and lay down. Then in the distance across the dark fields I saw a flame. With the rainy season, the fireflies had long since disappeared. What then could this be? The flame flickered, now brightly, now dimly, and sometimes it glowed like a halo, as if it had sunk deep into water.

I was frightened by this flame. For in my heart I, too, carried a flame.

One night it moved into the field where I was lying.

It hurried across the marsh, where duckweed and reeds grew rank, where no human being could possibly pass; as it approached, it oscillated at about the height of a paper lantern.

It seemed to be advancing in my direction. I tensed my body. Thereupon the flame swerved to the side, and following the line of the hills, rose slightly into the air and vanished.

I was at an utter loss. First I was just frightened; then I was angry.

🗦
🗦
🗦 28 🗦 *THE STARVING*
AND THE MAD

I ate plants and leeches to my heart's content. That my body could subsist on such fare was the result of my salt. It was because of my half pint or so of salt, which I licked in small quantities every day, that I was able, as I wandered over the rain-sodden fields and hills, to affirm to myself that I was still alive. When the salt finally gave out, my situation became truly desperate.

For some time now I had observed one peculiarity among the corpses by the roadside: like the bodies in the seaside village, they had been divested of the flesh on their buttocks. At first I had inferred by analogy that they also had been devoured by dogs and birds. One day, however, I noticed that just as the fireflies had disappeared from this mountainous country at the advent of the rainy season, so, too, had almost all other animals. I had seen neither snakes nor frogs, and the only birds I could hear were occasional turtledoves that warbled listlessly in the rare intervals between the rains.

How then could these dead people have lost their buttocks? My mind had dropped the habit of logical reasoning, and it was not until one day I happened to notice a body that still retained some trace of living suppleness and suddenly felt a desire to eat its flesh, that the answer dawned on me.

Yet I could not accept the idea that cannibalism had come to me as a natural instinct. Never, I thought, would it have occurred to me to alleviate my hunger in this way had I not heard the story of how the survivors of the *Medusa* ate each other on their raft, and later listened to reports of cannibalism on Guadalcanal and hints of the same practice from New Guinea. Anthro-

pology has, of course, clearly established that in prehistoric times people did eat each other, just as that
primitive societies practice incest; but for us who live
in the shadow of a long history and deeply rooted cus-
tom it is impossible without an access of abhorrence to
imagine fornicating with our mothers or eating human
flesh.

That I was now able to overlook such inveterate
prejudices must have been because I recognized in my
predicament an extreme exception to the normal human
condition. I cannot tell whether or not this new desire
of mine was natural; for I have forgotten what I really
felt at the time—just as lovers forget the exact feeling
that they experienced at a certain moment in their in-
tercourse.

What I do remember is that I hesitated, that I post-
poned the crucial instant. I also know the reason for
this. Each time I came across a new body I looked
round, for invariably I felt that I was being observed
by someone.

Who was observing me? It could not be that Filipino
woman. After all, I had not eaten her; I had only killed
her. . . .

I met another living person. From the way he walked

I could tell that there still was some resilience in his flesh. I understood the expression in his eyes when he stopped and looked me up and down as if to assess my body. He also appeared to understand my expression.

"Ee-e!" An inhuman sort of cry escaped his mouth as we passed each other.

One day I came across a group of men who had pitched their tent in the forest by the side of the road. They sat watching me with shining eyes as I passed.

"Ee-e!" This time the cry came from my side. I was not interested in them; I was on the lookout for immobile people—for fresh corpses that still retained human lineaments.

One evening when the rain had stopped and the crimson of the sky traced the hilltops I climbed one of the hills—perhaps so that I might more clearly view that crimson coloring. At the summit, leaning against a solitary tree, I found a single, motionless body.

Its eyes were closed. The sunrays as they moved down over the western hills shone on the green face and formed shadows in the recesses of the cheeks and chin. Then I perceived that the body was alive. The man opened his eyes. He seemed to be looking directly into the sun. His lips moved and words came forth.

"It's burning," he said. "It's burning! Quickly it's sinking, really quickly! The earth is turning around. That's why the sun is sinking, you know."

He looked at me. There was the same gleam in his eyes as I had seen when the soldier brushed past me with his cry of "Ee-e!"

"Where have you come from, fellow?" he said.

I sat down next to him, but did not answer. The sun hid itself in the hill opposite, and from between the trees that lined its summit the rays splashed forth in stripes. Only the clouds still shone golden as they hung in the sky. For some time they illuminated the two of us.

"The Western Paradise! Buddha is Amida. One is one. Two is two. I join my hands in prayer."

He put his hands together and on them leaned his bearded chin. With a rustling sound the rain began to fall.

"Uh, uh!" he said, lifting his face and laughing. He put back his head and let his mouth fall open to receive the raindrops. His throat rumbled. Only when he was actually swallowing did the sound of his voice cease entirely.

"Hey," I said, "let's leave here!"

"Leave? There's no reason to leave. A plane's coming to fetch me from Formosa. Don't you understand? They'll be landing right here by helicopter."

I looked at him. He was in his forties. His uniform, though discolored by sun and rain, showed him to be an officer; but he carried neither sword nor revolver.

"Uh, uh!" he kept saying. The movement of his chin whetted my appetite.

When the darkness covered our hilltop he finally grew silent. Then his stertorous breathing told me that he was asleep.

I did not sleep.

What first startled me in the morning light were the swarms of flies that covered the officer's face and hands. With a whistling sound of "Hee-e-e," he awoke. The flies buzzed off, as though frightened by the sound, and circled about a foot above him; occasionally they stopped in mid-air and the whirring of their wings became louder; then they settled on him once more.

He opened his eyes, swept the flies away, and bowed deeply.

"Your Imperial Majesty," he intoned, "Great Emperor of Japan, I humbly implore you to let me return home! Airplane, come and fetch me! Land here in a helicopter . . . Goodness, but it's dark," he broke off, lowering his voice. "So awfully dark! It's not yet morning."

"Certainly it's morning," I said. "Can't you hear the birds singing?"

It was a rainless morning. The busy voices of various types of birds came from the surrounding trees and from within the forest at the bottom of the valley. On the opposite hills I could see them darting back and forth like arrows in the spaces between the trees.

"Those aren't birds," said the officer. "They're ants! That's the buzzing of ants. You're a fool, you know!"

He grasped a handful of earth from between his knees and stuck it in his mouth. There was the smell of urine and excrement.

"Aha, aha!"

He closed his eyes. As though this was their signal, the flies closed in from far and near with a great whirring of wings. His face, his hands, his feet—every exposed part of his body was covered by swarms of murmuring insects.

They began to attack my body, too. I shook my hands, but they evidently made no distinction between me and the dying man—was I, in fact, dying too?—and my movements did not bother them in the slightest.

"It hurts! It hurts!" he said. Then from the sound of his regular breathing I gathered that he had fallen asleep again.

It began to pour. The rain streamed over the officer's body. The flies lost their foothold and slipped off one after another. In their place, large mountain leeches fell on him from the trees, accompanying the raindrops. Some that had landed a short distance away moved along the ground, folding their bodies up completely like cankerworms as they advanced on their prey.

"Your Imperial Majesty, Great Emperor of Japan," said the officer, bowing and shaking his head, from which the leeches dangled like tatters. I want to go home. Let me go home! Stop the war! Save us, O merciful Buddha! Buddha of mercy! I join my hands in prayer."

Yet once before he died he fixed me with the clear eyes of a policeman and in an access of lucidity, such as visits patients at the moment of their death, said: "What, are you still here? You poor fellow! When I'm dead, you may eat this."

Slowly he raised his emaciated left arm and slapped it with his other hand.

🐦

🐦

🐦 29 🐦 *THE HAND*

I turned the officer's body onto its face, and fixing the strap of my canteen around the chin, dragged it along the grass to a hollow a short way down the hill. Here I was well concealed by grass and shrubbery; no one could observe me.

Yet it was not as easy as I had imagined to put my plan into practice—the plan that I had so glibly conceived the day before on coming across this moribund madman. I was obsessed by the words that he had murmured before his death. For some reason these words, intended as an invitation, acted instead as a ban.

I rolled up the sleeve of the officer's shirt and stared at the upper arm that he himself had indicated. Emaciated though it was, I could tell that under its green skin were hidden the well-developed muscles of a military man. I remembered Jesus' arms, strained from hanging, which I had seen in the seaside village.

No sooner had I removed my hand from the arm than the flies swelled up on it. It was a relief to see the skin disappear from sight. Yet I could not tear myself away from the body.

When the rain started again the water brought with it the mountain leeches, who fought the flies for space on the officer's body. Even as I watched the great sucking worms grew fatter. Some of them dangled like eyelids from the lashes of the corpse's closed eyes.

I could not sit by watching idly while these black, rubbery spheres battened on my intended victim. I wrenched them off the corpse, crushed their swollen bodies, and sucked the blood with which they had gorged themselves.

It occurred to me then how illogical it was that though I could not bring myself to lay hands directly on my victim, I should have no compunction in drinking his blood through the medium of other living creatures. At this juncture the leeches were mere tools. What was the difference in principle between squeezing out the leeches, as I was now doing, and using some other instrument, specifically my bayonet, to rip open the flesh?

I had already killed one human being and thereby forfeited all hope of returning to the world of my fellow men: having with my own hands cut off the course of one human life, it would be intolerable to watch other people living.

Yet the death of the body that now lay at my feet was clearly not my fault, but that of the raging fever which had brought the madman's heart to a stop. Now that the officer's consciousness had finally ceased, he was no longer a human being. He did not differ, in fact, from the vegetables and animals we normally kill and eat without the slightest compunction.

What lay before me was a mere object—an object utterly unrelated to the soul that had uttered the words: "You may eat this."

I knelt down and began by plucking the leeches off the officer's arm. Soon a few inches of greenish skin lay exposed. I reflected that it was the same upper arm that he had granted me before his death (a fact which proves that even at this stage I must have retained some trace of sentimentality). With my right hand I drew my bayonet from its scabbard. Once more I glanced round to make sure no one was watching me.

Then a strange thing took place: I found that my left hand was firmly grasping the wrist of my right hand, the wrist that held my bayonet. This odd movement of my left hand was to become an ingrained habit: whenever I was about to eat something that I should not eat, my left hand would spring forward of its own accord; it would seize the wrist of the hand holding the fork and clasp it firmly until my errant appetite had vanished. I became so used to this habit that it seemed quite normal. At the time I felt that this living left hand of mine actually belonged to someone else.

My right hand, which during the thirty-odd years since I was born had been in charge of my daily tasks, had tough skin and thick joints; but my pampered and indolent left hand, long, limber, and beautiful, was the most conceited part of my whole body. As I gazed at the metacarpal bone, which protruded with the exertion of my left hand, I was for some time uncertain whether what I really wanted to eat was the flesh of the dead officer or this left hand of mine.

As I stood there in my strange pose I once again felt that I was being watched. Until the eyes left me I knew that I must not change my position.

"Let not thy left hand know what thy right hand doeth!"

The voice, when it came, did not particularly surprise me. After all, I had known all along that someone was watching me. Why should not this unseen person engage me in conversation?

It was not the primitive voice of the woman I had killed. No, it was that great, hollow voice which had called to me in the village church.

"Arise, I say unto thee, arise!" it boomed in my ears. And I stood up.

As I slowly moved away from the body my left hand loosened its grip—first the middle finger, then the ring finger, then the little finger, finally the thumb and the index finger together.

☙
☙
☙ 30 ☙ *THE LILIES OF*
THE FIELD

I went down the hill. The rain had stopped and the surrounding green sparkled freshly in the sunlight. As I walked through the forest and across the plain I was treading new land.

Everything was looking at me. The hill at the end of the plain gazed at me, revealing only that part of its body which lay above its breast. The trees vied with each other in coquetry to capture my attention. Even the blades of grass, decked with raindrops, raised their heads in greeting, or again, drooping their slender bodies, turned their faces in my direction.

Now and then the scene inclined to the left or to the right. As I moved forward through the sunlight I felt glad that I was being looked at. All the time vapor rose from my body. It came like flames from my hands, my hair, my uniform, and trailed behind me; gradually it rose, traveling upward until I felt that it would merge with the clouds above.

Iridescent and multiform were those clouds as they rode the winds, each at its own altitude, seething, twisting, scudding back and forth over the dazzling blue between me and the hills.

I came to a valley. This valley was familiar: it seemed that I had seen it many times before from a train window in Japan. The line of hills that bordered the railway line suddenly broke off and there, stretching far back into the distance, lay a valley with no roads across it. I had always enjoyed the sight of that valley; as the train approached it I used to look out of the window in expectation.

Yet surely the same valley could not exist here, thousands of miles away in the tropics! The trees on the hills that flanked it like gates and the grass that covered its gently rising floor naturally were different from those in the temperate climate of Japan. Yet for the life of me I could not but feel that this was one and the same valley. As I approached it the feeling grew within me that I was returning to a place where I had already been. Then I saw that the valley was looking at me.

The sunbeams flooded into the valley. Sitting down in the shade of the trees, I studied the vegetation. The plants themselves were dry, but the long tentacles of their roots, which spread over the entire floor of the valley, were washed in the noiselessly flowing water.

One of the plants stood out from the others. At the top of its straight stalk a tightly furled corolla was about to open up—gently, like a piece of music. It was an unknown tropical flower, something like a peony; inside, where the pink petals were folded, it was damp and the color was faded; there was no scent.

"You may eat me if you like!" said the flower abruptly, speaking in a woman's voice.

Then I realized that I was starving. I was about to pluck the flower when once again I found that my right and left hands were at cross-purposes. In fact, this time it was not only my hands, but the entire left and right sides of my body that felt like different entities; I knew then that it was the right side of my body, which included my right hand, that was starving.

My left side understood: it understood that though I had until now not hesitated to eat plants and bark and roots and leaves, it was in fact more wrong to eat these than dead people. For these were living things.

The flower still glistened in the sunlight. As I gazed

at it, it shone more and more brightly until the green of the surrounding grass receded and became dim.

Now from the sky flowers began to fall. Great masses of flowers, all of the same shape and size, gushed forth from the heavens, dropping down one after the other. They shone brightly as they fell, to converge eventually in the same peonylike plant.

"Consider the lilies of the field, how they grow; they toil not, neither do they spin. . . . If God so clothe the grass of the field, which to day is, and to morrow is cast into the oven, shall he not much more clothe you, O ye of little faith?"

The voice rose, opening up like a funnel above the flowers; it seemed to come from the flower-filled space above me. So this was God!

The glittering flowers continued to fall, but I knew that they would never reach me! There was no place for me within that pensile God—no place for this body of mine as it jerked its way between that great Being above and the earth below.

I tried to pray, but no prayer would thrust itself out of my mouth. For my body was sundered into two half-bodies.

My body must become transfigured.

31 THE FOWLS OF THE AIR

One day there was a rumbling in the air. It was a large formation of bombers crossing the narrow strip of sky above. They forced their way deeply through the blue sky, their wings spread out phoenixlike, and were hidden first by one cloud, then another. They roared past—yet with an illusion of slowness. Their noise filled the heavens, echoed off the ground, and thrust itself into my ears.

As they passed above me I felt that they were wounding God's body. One tardy plane was dyed half blue, half yellow.

Again I realized that I was starving.

Perhaps startled by the noise, a white heron flew up from a treetop across the valley. It stretched its neck, flapped its wings slowly, and rose skyward as if to catch up with the bombers.

Part of my body—the left-hand part—soared into the sky with the heron. I felt that my soul had left me and that I could no longer pray; now my right side was free to act as it wished.

Flies came down. They filled the whole sky, as the flowers had done before, and zoomed straight for my face, buzzing loudly. They were the blood of the wounded God.

I stood up, left the valley and, sharply conscious of my starvation, ran across the shining plain. Clinging to trees and grasping the roots of plants, I pulled my way painfully up the hill. And then in the hollow I saw *him* again, lying on his back.

He had become a colossus. On his swollen limbs, which had turned to a reddish brown, light-green patterns were traced like tattoos; a dirty-green substance oozed from the cracks in his skin; his distended stomach rose into two great globes, between which his leather cartridge belt formed a sort of boundary. He was inedible.

God had transformed him before my arrival. He was beloved of God. And I, too, perhaps. . . .

☙

☙

☙ 32 ☙ *THE EYES*

Yet if I, too, am beloved of God, why am I in this place?—why do I lie here stretched out on an unshaded river bed, broiled by the sun?

Will it never rain? The river has dried up and only the gentle undulations of the sand between the brown pebbles show where once the water flowed.

I look up at the cloudless sky and a coruscating flash of light explodes behind my eyeballs. I close my eyes.

Why do the flies come at me like this? They buzz around my head, then settle on my arid cheeks and start to creep about. With their great beaks they peck at the soft parts of my face—at my eyes, my nostrils, my mouth, my ears.

Why are my hands immobile, why will neither my right nor my left hand chase these flies away? My body feels torpid, but the reason is other than this.

Now that I have resolved in my heart never again to eat another living creature in order that I myself may live, I must resign myself to being eaten alive by these insects. That is why my hands refuse to drive them away as they swarm over my mucous membrane.

Just spare my eyes! Just leave me the joy of sight!

The joy of sight? What is the object that I see over there, glittering in the sun like a flower? Yes, it is a foot. Its five desiccated toes are spread out like the toes of a chicken's foot. It has been severed about two inches above the ankle. In the center of the cut the bone gleams white like the pistil of a flower. The ends of the skin seem to be folded over and the flesh beneath is ebony-black. Its swollen surface shakes and shimmers like a lotus floating on the waves. Ah, yes, now I can see: that seething black surface is a cluster of jostling flies.

It looks like a human foot. Yet why should a severed human foot suddenly appear before my eyes? No, no, it was not I who cut it off! This is not *his* foot. His is rotten and bloated, but the one before me is still fairly fresh and has the proper indentations between its phalanxes. The place, too, is different: *he* lies in the hollow of a hill, while I, I . . . why am I here in this river bed?

Who, then, can have cut off the foot? Why should just one foot have been washed up like a fish on this bright river bed?

No, I do not want to eat it. It is for me to be eaten—by the flies.

Then why is the foot advancing in my direction?

Shaking, shining, laughing, it comes over the dry earth toward me.

I know this feeling. It is the feeling that I had when I crawled as a baby. I do not remember the sense of muscular tension in my arms and legs, but only the smiling face of my mother, the goal of my exertions, as she seems to approach me, swaying slightly.

So now again I am crawling—but this time toward a severed human foot. An unpleasant smell, like that of my own perspiration, approaches. Someone is watching.

I summon up my last reserves of strength and roll my body over on its side. Once, twice, three times I roll around. Still it is not enough. The sand comes to an end and I reach the shade where the rushes are clustered together. Once more round, twice more. . . .

No, I did not merely imagine that I was being watched. Now I have actually seen the eyes.

There they are, between the dark tree trunks of the forest about twenty yards ahead across the field of mottled rushes—two eyes, gleaming like the eyes of a Buddha in a miniature shrine.

Not two eyes only; for below them I can now see a sharply delineated white circle, and in its center another perfect circle, hollow and black as a cave—a circle of steel. It is the muzzle of a rifle.

Like an animal I put my ear to the dry earth and wait for a sound. The sound approaches. It is not the sound of shoes, but that of feet stepping stealthily over pebbles and sand. Yes, it is the sound of feet carrying the weight of a human being as he treads the globe.

Finally he appears. He pushes aside the rushes and stands there looking down at me.

The long dishevelled hair, the jaundiced cheeks, the beard that straggles down at random, the lids that cover a pair of drowsy eyeballs—he is unlike any human being that I have seen.

This being gives vent to words. He even utters my name.

"Aren't you Tamura?"

His voice reaches my ears as if from the other side of a wall. Before gathering the import of his words, I observe how his mouth moves, to display a set of dirty, irregular teeth; I look at him with the indifference that I might feel for the movements of some unfamiliar animal.

"Aren't you Tamura?" says the mouth once more.

I gaze up at him and grope in my memory for his

identity. Instead, his features become blurred. No, surely I have never met this old man before! Can it by any chance be God? I dismiss the possibility; God must be much bigger.

His tattered clothes still retain the general color and shape of a Japanese soldier's uniform.

"Nagamatsu!"

I hear myself call out the name of that young soldier whom I met in front of the hospital. Then everything turns dark before my eyes.

🐦
🐦
🐦   33   🐦   *FLESH*

I felt a coolness running up my shins and returned to myself. Next to me was Nagamatsu's face. His hands were supporting my head and water was splashing over me. He was laughing.

"Pull yourself together!" he said. "It's water."

I snatched the canteen from his hands and drank it dry at a single draught. Still I was thirsty. Nagamatsu eyed me intently, and taking from his haversack a black, biscuitlike object, thrust it into my mouth without a word.

It had the taste of dry cardboard. When I had eaten several of the objects, however, I realized that it was meat. It was dry and hard, but with it came a taste that I had not experienced once in all the months since I had left my unit; a taste of grease permeated my mouth.

An ineffable sorrow pierced me. So I had gone back on all my resolves and interdictions! No sooner had I met a companion and received the benefits of his friendship, than I had begun eating without demur the forbidden flesh. And the meat was delicious! My teeth had become fantastically weak and I had to suck at the hard slabs, but even as I did so I could feel that strength was being given to me. At the same time something was being taken away.

The left and right sides of my body became sated and once more were joined together.

I looked questioningly at Nagamatsu, who glancing away, answered: "It's monkey's meat."

"Monkey's?"

"Yes, I shot it the other day in the forest over there and put it out to dry."

I studied Nagamatsu's face out of the corner of my eyes. Now for the first time it had dawned on me that the pair of eyes and the rifle muzzle I had seen through the trees belonged to none other than him. Even here in the clear sunlight I now and then seemed to distinguish under his drooping lids the gleam of a Buddha's eyes.

"Tell me," I said, "you didn't by any chance mistake me for a monkey?"

He laughed loudly.

"Good Lord, no! But you were certainly rolling around like some sort of animal! I wonder what got into you. It's a good thing I recognized you so quickly. . . . Well, anyhow, you'd better try to stand up. Think you can make it?"

"I don't know."

He put his hands under my arms and helped me to my feet. My stomach was clogged with the meat that I had gulped down, and I felt as if a metal rod had been thrust into my body.

Now that I was standing, the river bed seemed much broader.

"The foot, the foot!" I said.

"Foot? What foot?"

"There's a foot right over there. It's been cut off at the ankle. It's rolled into the river bed."

Again I was conscious of that stench, similar to the stench of the decomposed corpses in the seaside village.

"It's foul," I cried, "it's unbearable!"

"Yes, it's pretty bad," said Nagamatsu.

"Don't you know anything about it?"

"Of course not."

"It's right over there."

"Yes, I see. Some soldier must have got his foot shot clean off at the ankle."

I had a moment's misgiving.

"What about your friend?" I asked.

"Yasuda? Oh, he's all right. He'll be very pleased to see you. Come on—let's get going!"

Exerting all his strength, the young soldier helped me along. As we threaded our way through the sparse rushes and approached the forest the smell still did not abate.

"Is this where you came from just now?" I asked him.

"That's right. We've got our camp here in the forest. It's not much of a camp, of course, but at least it's somewhere to sleep."

A well-trampled path led at a slight incline into the forest. The branches on both sides had been chopped to the length of firewood and hung up to dry, a method current in Filipino settlements. Abruptly Nagamatsu bent down and picked up an object. With a shudder I recognized it as a rifle—no doubt the same rifle he had pointed at me between the trees. Yet afterwards he had given me meat and water and now he was helping me to walk: surely this contradicted my suspicions.

I lacked the courage to follow up my doubts by questioning Nagamatsu. Since eating the monkey flesh I had felt that things must take their own course.

"Have you any bullets left?" I said nonchalantly.

"Yes, I've still got a few. I haven't been wasting any. But when these are used up I don't know how we're going to get enough food to keep going."

"Have you been here all along?"

"Oh, yes. Yasuda can't move an inch, you see. They say there are Americans on the Ormoc Highway, but we can't possibly get that far."

"Even if you did, you couldn't get across."

"That isn't what's worrying us. We'd just stick our hands up, as Yasuda's been planning all along. After all, if we stay here, we're both of us done for. But the old geezer can't do much walking with those ulcers of his."

"It's wonderful the way you've been looking after him all this time," I said.

"Pooh, I'd be lonely by myself! Besides, he's got the tobacco."

"Still?"

"Yes, he's a tightfisted bastard, all right! The only time he'll fork out any of the stuff is when I shoot a monkey and bring it to him. The funny thing is he doesn't smoke even a puff himself."

The forest gradually became denser and the sunlight no longer penetrated the covering of branches. There was a damp coolness in the air. Amidst the chirping of the birds I could hear shouts of "Hey, hey, there!"

"You see," said Nagamatsu, "that's Yasuda calling me. When I'm not there he's as helpless as a child. Yet the old bastard is as bossy as ever. . . . Hey!" shouted Nagamatsu in reply as the sound of Yasuda's voice came closer.

We pushed our way through a thicket and emerged into a small clearing, which was backed by the face of a steep hill. The earth had been dug to make a small, square hearth; on it was burning a fire. Under a piece of canvas, whose corners had been roughly fixed to four trees, sat Yasuda, his swollen leg still stretched in front of him.

His eyes protruded like a bird's; his hair and beard had grown at random and had taken on a brownish tint. He seemed to be nonplused by my presence.

"It's Tamura," Nagamatsu said.

Yasuda opened his eyes still wider and glared at

his companion without speaking a word. Looking aside, the latter squatted down beside him.

"I'm sorry," I said.

Yasuda had a wry look on his face, but his voice was unexpectedly gentle as he answered me.

"That's fine . . . fine. Now tell me how this all happened."

"Nagamatsu found me lying over there in the river bed. I'd collapsed."

"Hm. He found you, did he? I see. Well, Tamura, I've now got to the point where I can't move even an inch by myself. I depend entirely on the meat that Nagamatsu brings me. Otherwise I'd starve to death. How about it—is the war over yet?"

"Don't be silly," said Nagamatsu. "How d'you expect Tamura to know? He's been wandering around in the dark just as we have."

"Hm. Got any food with you, Tamura?"

I shook my head. Now I understood the reproachful look that Yasuda had thrown his companion: in this camp I would be no more than an extra stomach.

"I haven't got a thing," I said. "I've just been living on grass and mountain leeches."

Confused memories sprang up within me, memories of that vague period through which I had passed. Could

God be hovering about here also—in this isolated forest clearing? I raised my hand to touch His great body, but my extended fingers felt only a gentle breeze.

"Don't you even have a rifle?" Yasuda's voice reached my ears.

"No. But I do have a hand grenade."

"Grenade!" they shouted in unison.

Surprised at this reaction, I felt about for the grenade in my belt. No, no sign of it! Then I remembered that after the rains had begun I had slipped it into my haversack for safekeeping. Furtively I felt for it. Yes, there it was—bulky, heavy, lying on its side at the bottom of my bag. About to tell them, at the last moment I stopped myself. Something in their voices must have warned me.

"I suppose I've gone and dropped it," I said.

"What a hell of a waste!" said Yasuda. "There's a pond over there and if you throw a grenade in you can land all the fish you want."

"Don't you have one either?" I asked.

"No, I've used mine. All we've got now is Nagamatsu's rifle. So long as he can find a few monkeys to shoot, we'll keep going," said Yasuda and laughed noiselessly, displaying his teeth. Like all those I had seen on the island, they were irregular and decayed.

ᴪ
ᴪ
ᴪ 34 ᴪ *HUMANKIND*

As the day was drawing to a close, the fire in the hearth glowed more brightly. Yasuda and Nagamatsu each took some dried monkey flesh out of their haversacks and placed it on a rack above the hearth. Yasuda took out one piece, Nagamatsu two; of the latter, one was my share.

"Hey, how many pieces does that leave us with?" said Yasuda.

"Not very many," Nagamatsu answered.

"I asked you how many."

"What's the difference? We're sticking to our decision not to eat more than three a day, aren't we? Stop fussing and hand over the tobacco!"

"I'll give you the tobacco all right. But you're going to have to work a lot harder at that hunting of yours! We've got an extra mouth to feed from now on, haven't we?"

Nagamatsu was silent. It was the first time that I had seen him fail to answer Yasuda.

Yasuda clicked his tongue and looked at me peevishly.

A broad leaf like a bog rhubarb was cooking in a mess tin. Yasuda and Nagamatsu broke off a piece each, chewed it, and spat it out. Accustomed as I was to eating raw plants, I swallowed my portion.

"If you want to get the gripes," said Yasuda, "you're going just the right way about it!"

When our meal was over, Nagamatsu took a tobacco leaf from his pocket, carefully tore off a piece, and rolled it into the form of a cigarette, using a sheet of lined paper which he must have preserved carefully for this purpose. Then he began smoking. After each puff he raised the cigarette to his head with an air of reverent gratitude. There was a look of satisfaction on Yasuda's face as he observed the young man smoking.

"Funny thing, isn't it, Tamura? I wonder what's so wonderful about tobacco. Everyone knows it's pure poison for the system. People who smoke are a bunch of fools, aren't they?"

"I suppose so."

There was a peculiar tickling sensation in my throat. I expected Nagamatsu to offer me a puff, but instead he finished his cigarette, collected the dirty mess tins, and disappeared into the darkness, evidently in order to wash them in a near-by spring.

Being left alone face to face with Yasuda was vaguely

disagreeable. If God had not been there observing me, I doubt whether I could have stood it.

"I'm sorry," I said. "When I can move about a bit better, I'll help look for food."

"It's all right," said Yasuda, "it's quite all right. Anyhow, the way things are going now, I don't expect we'll be around all that long!"

Nagamatsu returned with the canteens, which he had filled with water.

"There you are," he said, placing one of them next to Yasuda and keeping the other in his hand. "Well, Tamura, are you ready to turn in?"

"What, don't we all sleep here?" I said

"My quarters are over there," answered Nagamatsu. "Come along!"

I was drowsy and felt quite ready to go to sleep where I was.

"I'm all right here," I said.

"Come along!" insisted Nagamatsu. "It's just over there."

"If he says he's all right," remarked Yasuda testily, "why the hell can't he stay here?"

"Look, Tamura, you'd better listen to me!" said Nagamatsu. "Yasuda's leg gets bad at night. He'll just keep you awake with his groaning. Come on!"

He lifted me to my feet. Yasuda turned over on his side.

Supported by Nagamatsu, I hobbled along through the darkness. As soon as we were out of earshot, I asked Nagamatsu:

"What's the trouble? Why don't you two sleep in the same place?"

"You'll understand soon enough. When things get to this point, you can't even trust your best friend. Look here, I've brought you along with me, haven't I? That's because I can trust you more than I can Yasuda."

I was silent.

"About your grenade," he continued. "You'd better see that Yasuda doesn't get his hands on it. Ammunition—that's the one thing we've really got to be careful about!"

"You seem to be very sure that I've still got my grenade, don't you?"

Nagamatsu laughed. "If I couldn't catch on to something as simple as that, I don't know where I'd be! Can't you see where I've got my arm?"

He tapped playfully on my haversack.

Nagamatsu's "quarters" were in a hollow about forty yards from the hill where Yasuda was lying. He had made a thatched shelter of rushes supported by bamboo props. In one corner was a neat pile of empty tins, interiors of gas masks, and other military paraphernalia; there was also a heavy, rough sword.

"Quite a weapon!" I said.

"That's what I cut the monkeys up with when I've caught them. Look, here's what I sharpen it with." He pointed to a piece of coarse natural sandstone.

"Mind you don't go and tell Yasuda about this place! He makes an awful fuss about that leg of his, but I don't believe for a second that he can't walk. If he finds out where I am, there's no telling what he mightn't do while I'm asleep. That's why I won't sleep where he does. See what I mean? I can't have him walking off with my rifle or something, can I?"

"But why should he want to take your rifle?"

"Oh well, you'll understand."

It occurred to me then that I should perhaps also be on my guard against Nagamatsu; yet I could not imagine what particular danger to look for. Exhausted from walking and from finally having proper food in my stomach, I fell asleep at once.

🐾 35 🐾 *THE MONKEYS*

At daybreak it began to rain. Nagamatsu had judiciously constructed his roof at a slant and had also dug a rain trench: so we managed to keep dry.

"Raining, isn't it?" said Nagamatsu, clicking his tongue irritably against the roof of his mouth. He stood up. "Come on, Tamura, let's be off."

"Is the fire going to be all right?"

"Don't worry about the fire. That's Yasuda's job."

To be sure, when we reached his tent, Yasuda was already busy preserving the precious fire. Having put some embers into his mess tin, he covered them with the lid, leaving just enough space on top so that they would not be smothered.

"It's begun raining, hasn't it?" he said, glaring up at Nagamatsu.

"I suppose that's my fault!"

"You won't be able to bag any monkeys, will you?"

"I expect a few will be coming along, even if it is raining. . . . Well, I might as well be going. Tamura, you stay here."

"I'll come with you," I said.

"No, I'll manage by myself all right," said Nagamatsu. "You still can't walk properly. When you're a
little better, you can come along and help me. . . . Be
careful," he added under his breath, and stepped out
into the rain.

Once more I was left alone with Yasuda. We sat in
silence under his piece of canvas. The rain dripped in.
I felt ill at ease.

"I'm still sleepy," I said. "I think I'll go back to
Nagamatsu's place and have a nap."

"Oh, aren't you all right here?" said Yasuda, suddenly becoming affable. "Why don't you have your nap
here? Look, there's a good dry place for you to sleep.
Lie down, make yourself at home! You know, Tamura,
I feel a lot more comfortable since you've joined us
here. That Nagamatsu fellow has become so damned
pleased with himself lately. He's got to oppose me on
every single thing! He didn't use to be like that. If I
hadn't been there to look after him, by now he'd be
lying stone dead somewhere by the side of the road. I
even taught the young oaf how to catch monkeys."

"Are there that many monkeys around here?" I asked.
"I haven't seen a single one myself."

"Well, there aren't such a lot," answered Yasuda.
"Just enough to keep us going, that's all. But now with

this rain, the damned creatures probably won't come out of their lairs."

Presently Nagamatsu returned.

"It's hopeless today," he said. "But the rainy season should be just about over."

"Do you know what date it is?" I asked.

"Yes," said Yasuda, "I've been keeping an exact record. It's the tenth of February. The rains should be over by the end of the month."

I was astounded. The abortive attempt to break through the Ormoc Highway had been at the beginning of January: since then I must have been wandering about by myself for over a month.

Despite Yasuda's prediction, the rainy season gave no sign of coming to an end. Nagamatsu no longer went out to hunt and our ration of meat decreased slightly each day. Now we did not bother to join Yasuda under his canvas, but brought some kindling charcoal to Nagamatsu's place and made our own fire. All day long I would sit opposite Nagamatsu, hugging my knees. He used to look at me with a grim expression.

"It was quite something of me to bring you here!" he said one day. "Mind you don't forget it!" The supply of meat had given out.

One morning it finally stopped raining and Nagamatsu went out to try his luck. For the first time in weeks I walked over to where Yasuda was lying.

"If he doesn't manage to catch anything today," I said, "I'll try going myself. Where's that pond—the one you said I could catch fish in with my hand grenade?"

"That was ages ago. Anyhow, it's miles away somewhere. Did you say hand grenade? I thought you'd lost yours."

"As a matter of fact, I've still got it—in my haversack."

"Eh?" said Yasuda, looking at me with wide-open eyes. "Well, but it's probably got wet through in all this rain. Come on, let's have a look."

Without thinking, I took the grenade out of my bag and handed it to him.

"Hm, it's a ninety-nine, isn't it? Let's see, I wonder if it's properly set. Yes, it looks as if it's still all right."

What he did then was unexpected: as if it were the most natural thing in the world, he stuffed the grenade into his haversack and tightly fastened the cord.

"Hey," I said, "give it back!"

"Well, now," said Yasuda, "I don't really mind letting you have it back, but what does it matter who keeps it? Why don't you let me look after it for you? After all, I never budge from here, do I? I'm in the best position to look after things. If you keep it, you'll just get it wet again. That would never do, would it?"

I began to feel uneasy.

"Give it back anyway," I said. "I'll see that it doesn't get wet. Nagamatsu will be angry if I let you keep it."

"Why, did he say something?"

"He said I shouldn't let you have it."

"Aha! In that case why did you give it to me?"

"I wasn't thinking."

"Well, that was your big mistake, wasn't it? It's too late now, though. No use crying over spilled milk!"

"Give it back, I say!"

As I stretched out my hand for Yasuda's haversack he drew out his bayonet. I jumped back. I, too, had a bayonet, but it seemed absurd for the two of us alone here in the middle of the forest to cross swords over a single hand grenade.

"All right," I said, "keep it. If you want it so badly, you can have it. But put that bayonet away this minute!"

"Good. I'm glad to see the intelligentsia living up to its reputation for getting the point quickly! Well, if you really want to give it to me, I won't object."

The time seemed to have come for me to set out for the hunting grounds. Yet for a moment I hesitated. I stared at my hands. I heard a voice: "Behold my hands which have not worked."

There was a bang in the distance.

"He's got one!" shouted Yasuda.

I rushed out and ran through the forest in the direction of the shot. Presently I reached a spot where the trees grew sparsely and from where I could see across the river bed. A human form was flying over its sun-drenched surface! His hair was in disorder and he was barefoot. It was a Japanese soldier in a green uniform. And it was not Nagamatsu!

Again there was the report of a gun. The bullet went wide of its apparent mark and the crouched figure continued running. He ran steadily along the river bed, now and then glancing back over his shoulder. Then, evidently confident that he was out of range, he gradually straightened his back and slowed down to a walking pace. Finally he disappeared into a clump of trees.

Now I had seen one of the "monkeys." I had, of course, expected this.

I walked to the part of the river bed where I had originally come across the severed foot. As I approached the rushes the smell became more and more pungent. Then I came to a spot where there were many feet.

But not only feet! Every part of the human anatomy

that was gastronomically useless had been amputated and thrown away in this place. Here they lay in a heap —hands, feet, heads—transformed in fullest measure by the baking of the sun and the saturation of the rain. The great putrid mess that rose before me defies all efforts at description.

Yet if I were to say that I was shocked by the sight, I should be exaggerating. Human beings are capable of receiving new impressions, however anomalous; at such moments one often views things with astonishing objectivity and this acts as a sort of shock absorber.

I was not surprised at all that here where my fate had led me such things should exist. Nor was I in the least frightened by the prospect of having to live with this new knowledge. For there was a God.

One thing only was needful: my body must be transfigured.

🦋

🦋

🦋 36 🦋 *IN PRAISE OF TRANSFIGURATION*

"Hey, come back here!" shouted someone.

I turned around and saw Nagamatsu standing at the edge of the forest, aiming his rifle at me. I smiled. Now I had to act a part: I made a pretense of grasping the grenade I no longer possessed and of being about to throw it.

"All right, all right," shouted Nagamatsu, "I understand!"

He laughed and lowered his rifle. As we approached each other, I saw that his cheek muscles were twitching.

"Did you see?" he said.

"Yes, I saw."

"You've eaten it too, you know."

"I knew that," I answered him.

"He got away—that monkey."

"Too bad!"

"I don't know when I'll find another. There aren't many monkeys passing this way," said Nagamatsu.

Then he saw that my hand was empty.

"Hey, what's happened to your grenade?"

"I haven't got it."

"You haven't got it?" he said.

"That's right. I was only pretending I had it."

"What's happened to it?"

"Yasuda took it from me."

"Took it from you?" said Nagamatsu, flushing violently. "You damned idiot, how could you let him take it when I specially warned you?"

"I wasn't thinking."

"What a hell of a situation! Well, it can't be helped now. I'll just have to get rid of the fellow, that's all. If I don't, he'll get me!"

"Why not get rid of me?"

"If I'd wanted to, I'd have done it right away. Anyhow, I'm fed up with this sort of thing. That bastard over there got me under his thumb, and before I knew it, I'd started. But I've had enough now. . . . Tell me, do you know the way to the Ormoc road?"

"I don't remember."

"Well, anyhow, we'll get there together. I'll finish off Yasuda, and when we've had our meal we'll go and find the Americans. All right?"

"It's not all that easy to surrender," I said, realizing with a jolt what the only possible contents of the meal could be.

"Anyhow, I've had enough of being pushed around by that old bastard, and that's that! I'm certainly not going to leave things as they are."

"Why not just clear out?" I asked him.

"That's no good. Right now I haven't any food."

"But I'm not going to surrender, you know! You can go by yourself. I don't feel like it."

"Don't be silly. You aren't the only one who's been eating monkey meat. If we keep our mouths shut, how's anyone going to find out?"

The method that Nagamatsu had devised for killing his newly armed companion was of a cunning that belied his youth. According to his calculations, Yasuda would certainly try to kill us now that he had laid hands on a weapon; with this in mind, he would by now have left his tent and be lying somewhere in wait for us.

"He exaggerates about that damned leg of his—he can use it perfectly well if he wants to," Nagamatsu said. "He only pretends that he can't so that I'll keep my nose to the grindstone!"

Cautiously we entered the forest.

"The thing to do is to make him use the grenade," remarked Nagamatsu. "If I shout, he'll be sure to throw it at me. So the minute I call out, we'll run for our lives. See?"

Making a trumpet of his hands, Nagamatsu shouted at the top of his lungs: "Hey, Yasuda! I've bagged him!" At once he turned on his heels and ran. I followed suit. We had not made twenty yards when behind us there was a tremendous explosion. A clump of small trees by the spot where we had been standing was flung high in the sky. As I lagged behind the young man, a fragment of the grenade tore a piece from my shoulder. I quickly picked up the morsel, wiped off the dirt, and popped it in my mouth. There could certainly be nothing wrong in eating my own flesh.

After that we started to look for Yasuda. We spent half the day in an assiduous search, but he was nowhere to be found.

"Damn it all," said Nagamatsu, "where the hell can he have got to?" No doubt hunger was his impelling motive, but mixed with this was an element of hatred.

"I've got it!" he cried suddenly. "That's the place all right."

He led me to a spring.

"This is the only place where there's any water. The old bastard's bound to come this way before long. We'll just sit and wait for him."

At the bottom of the hill by the edge of the trees water gushed into the open, formed a rivulet, and meandered between the trees. Nagamatsu dammed up the flow with a large stone.

We hid ourselves on a knoll that commanded the spring. On the evening of the third day we heard Yasuda's voice approaching from the distance. He sounded plaintive.

"Nagamatsu! Tamura!" he shouted. "Hey, fellows, come on out! I know I'm in the wrong, but let's make it up. . . . I've got a good fire going, you know!"

"As far as fires go," shouted Nagamatsu, "we've got one here ourselves." He blew on the small embers he had stored in his mess tin.

"Come on out!" said Yasuda. "You can have all my tobacco."

"You're wasting your breath! I've had enough of your charity, thank you. As soon as I've finished you off, I'll take all the tobacco I want without waiting to be invited!"

"Come out! If you think I've got my tobacco with me, you're making a big mistake. I've got it hidden safely away. Come on, let's be friends again!"

"Damn you, you crafty old swine!" said Nagamatsu, grinding his teeth.

Finally the voice stopped. Now there was only the sound of someone crawling through the underbrush.

Presently a head appeared over the top of the hill beyond the spring. For a while it stayed there motionless, then the whole body emerged and Yasuda slid down to the bottom of the hill.

Nagamatsu had already raised his rifle, pointing directly in Yasuda's direction. When he fired, Yasuda's body moved convulsively, then fell on the ground and lay still.

Nagamatsu dashed over to it. With his bayonet he quickly chopped through the wrists and ankles. The most horrible thing of all was that I had been expecting these very actions!

I approached the body. With Yasuda's cherry-red flesh before my eyes, I vomited. My empty stomach brought forth only a yellowish liquid.

If at this time God had already transfigured my body, glory be to God!

I was seized with anger: if as a result of hunger human beings were constrained to eat each other, then this world of ours was no more than the result of God's wrath. And if I at this moment could vomit forth anger, then I, who was no longer human, must be an angel of God, an instrument of God's wrath.

I jumped to my feet, and as though propelled by some

supernatural force, hurried up the slope above the spring and towards the rifle with which Nagamatsu had shot his companion.

The young man's voice followed me: "Wait a minute, Tamura! Wait a minute! I know what you're going to do."

His legs seemed to have acquired a new vitality as they ran in pursuit of me, far faster than my own. I was only a pace ahead of him when I reached the rifle he had so carelessly left there on the ground.

Nagamatsu opened his red mouth and laughingly grasped the barrel of the rifle, which I aimed at him. But he was too late.

I do not remember whether I shot him at that moment. But I do know that I did not eat his flesh; this I should certainly have remembered.

My next memory is an image of the forest seen from the distance. It was dark, like a Japanese cedar wood, and there was an insensate quality about the surroundings. It was hateful to me.

Closing in on the forest, the rain began to fall quietly, like water pouring down a stained-glass window.

I gazed at the rifle in my hand. It was a requisitioned 25-caliber rifle like the one I had had before, and the Imperial chrysanthemum crest had been crossed out with a large X. I took a cloth from my pocket and wiped off the raindrops that had spattered on the cover of the breechblock.

It is here that my memory breaks off.

A Madman's Diary

I am writing this in the room of a mental home on the outskirts of Tokyo. On the lawn outside my window some of the less serious patients are standing about in little groups, basking in the weak autumn sun. The tall red pines that surround the hospital glitter in the sunlight and look down on the segregated inmates.

Six years have passed since that time on Leyte Island. My memory, which breaks off at the point where I was wiping the cover of my breechblock, begins again in the American field hospital at Ormoc. I had suffered a contusion on the back of my head. It was the pain of the resetting operation for my cranial fracture that brought me back to myself; from then on, I gradually recovered my power of perception and my memory.

I had no idea how I had received my wound or by what means I had reached the hospital. According to one of the American orderlies, I had been captured in the mountains by Filipino guerrillas; it was at that time, no doubt, that I had been wounded. The Army doctor explained to me that my loss of memory was a simple case of retrograde amnesia caused by cerebral concussion.

Apart from loss of hair, I had suffered no superficial damage. My heart, however, had undergone a functional lesion, and for over two months after being moved to the special P.O.W. hospital at Tacloban, I was unable to walk as far as the toilet. The pneumonic infiltration, which had caused me to be thrown out of my unit, had also advanced. I was kept in an isolation ward with other consumptive patients, and without being transferred to a general P.O.W. camp, was repatriated on a hospital ship in March of 1946.

From when I was first admitted to the P.O.W. hospital, I had attracted the attention of the other patients in my ward by performing a sort of ritual at the dining table to which I was assigned. They looked on me as insane. Yet I can see nothing shameful in this habit of mine—a habit that indeed I have kept until this day. Forced on me as it is by some power outside myself, it is not my responsibility.

Whenever I eat food composed of organic matter, though I know full well that I am only eating in order to preserve my own life, I begin by apologizing to the organism to whom this matter originally belonged.

Far from regretting my habit, I feel that the strange people are those who, though they rant about love for their fellow creatures, about magnanimity—in fine, about their humanism—can at the same time feed on organic matter without the slightest self-reproach.

When one day I abruptly gave up my ritual, it was because it seemed immaterial whether or not I practiced it. What interested me now was to hide my feelings from others.

I informed no one about what I had experienced since leaving my company. I was frightened that if my murder of the Filipino woman should come to light, I might be indicted as a war criminal; also I could not tell what the other prisoners might think of my having shot a comrade, even if they knew that he had turned cannibal.

It was not that I sought to cling avidly to life, but simply that having once entered into this serene existence at the hospital, I had no reason to go out of my way to interrupt it. After all, people live only because they have no reason to die. Besides, I knew that since I was still alive, I must conform to the preposterous rules of my fellows. I had a wife at home.

She received me with delight, and I, too, seeing her joyous face, was filled with joy. Yet our relationship had changed. In general I can say that the cause was my strange experiences in the Philippine mountains. True, what I had done was of no account: I had killed people, but I had not eaten them. The fact remained that I had memories my wife could not share; it was these memories that now, to use the lame metaphor, "came between" us.

An irrepressible desire to be alone has persisted since my return. When my wife told me the story of how during one of the air raids on Tokyo our house was hemmed in by flames and she was only rescued by a miracle, I muttered the conventional expressions of gratification. Yet to my amazement the thought that had really occurred to me was that she would have done better to die at that time.

I did not feel like repressing and denying all my true thoughts. When, five years after my return, I resumed the ceremony of bowing in front of the dining table, and once more began to refuse all sorts of food, I was not inclined to regard this behavior as strange or to give it up. Nor could I help the fact that now my left hand would again stretch out to grasp my right hand; for I was being impelled by something outside myself—by God, perhaps. Certainly, were I not being moved from the outside, I should never have resumed these habits.

When one day in May I visited this mental home and saw the building buried in the gentle green of the Japanese oak trees, so similar to the green of the Philippine hills, I realized that I had come to the proper place and I only regretted not having known about it sooner. Then I decided to become an inmate, and finally the time came when I stood inside of the heavy doors and my wife outside. In her tear-filled eyes I could feel the weight of the heart I had killed. But who am I to worry about killing a heart? Am I not he who killed bodies?—many bodies?

Moreover, I am aware that my wife's heart is not her whole existence. That we are all split into many parts, I, a madman, know from my own experience. Between human beings, who within themselves are already so divided, how can there really be such a thing as love, whether it be love between husband and wife or between parent and child?

Now I want to have things done for me just as I wish. To make me abandon one of my wishes, it is necessary to act as the officer in the Philippine mountains and to offer me the thing *before* I want it. My desires are extremely few: they must be forestalled before I am conscious of them. At the same time, no one can make me do what I do not want to do.

It struck me as strange that the broken life I had to patch up on my return to Japan tended to make me do only things that I did not wish to do.

The reports in the newspapers, which reach me morning and evening even in this secluded spot, seem to be trying to force me into the thing that I want least of all, namely, another war. Wars may be advantageous to the small group of gentlemen who direct them, and I therefore leave these people aside; what baffles me is all the other men and women who now once again seem so anxious to be deluded by these gentlemen. Perhaps they will not understand until they have gone through experiences like those I had in the Philippine mountains; then their eyes will be opened.

But I must not let my fears run away with me. After all, the reports in the newspapers are only symptoms. A single symptom makes a transient impression and is soon forgotten. What makes symptoms take root in our consciousness is that they appear intermittently or periodically—just as on the island what made me fear the fires in the plains was the *order* in which they appeared and their *number*. If indeed the symptoms in the newspapers are the work of mass-psychologists playing on the public mind, then my hatred goes out to those experts.

Yet the revolutionaries who aim to abolish this system can contrive only the most inane policies, and instead of working together, persist in their petty squabbles. They need not expect to see me risking my life at the barricades as a cog in the fulfillment of their plans—any more than certain gentlemen need expect to force me once more onto their battlefields. No one in the future can make me do what is hateful to me. . . .

I realize that all this is a mere farrago of nonsense. Since I reluctantly returned to this world everything has become voluntary. Before I entered the war, my life was founded on individual necessity and what happened was, for me at least, inevitable. Yet after I had once been exposed on the battlefield to the arbitrariness of authority, it all turned to chance. My return to Japan was based on chance and my present existence, being the result of my repatriation, is likewise based on chance. Were it not for the chance of having been sent home, I should not even be seeing that wooden chair in the corner of my room.

People seem unable to admit this principle of chance. Our spirits are not strong enough to stand the idea of life being a mere succession of chances—the idea, that is, of infinity. Each of us in his individual existence, which is contained between the chance of his birth and the chance of his death, identifies those few incidents that have arisen through what he styles his "will"; and the thing that emerges consistently from this he calls his "character" or again his "life." Thus we contrive to comfort ourselves; there is, in fact, no other way for us to think.

Yet perhaps this, too, is all nonsense. My life in this mental home is spent in gazing at the movements of the heavenly bodies—at the sun, the moon, the stars, the earth—and day after day it is interrupted by sleep. My doctor has allotted me a daily assignment of cleaning and tidying my room; this is a good thing, for while I am engaged in it I can forget the principle of chance. . . .

There is a certain irony in the fact that the attendants here are mostly orderlies from the defunct Japanese Army. I find it pleasant to recall their past careers from the way in which they occasionally strike the patients: it makes for a certain bond between my present existence and my life on the front.

The method (if indeed one exists) of transforming into necessity the chance that dominates my present life probably lies in finding the link between this life and that past in which chance was forced on me by authority. It is for this reason that I am writing these notes.

Once More to the Fires on the Plain

It was on the recommendation of my doctor that I originally began writing. Apparently he considered it a suitable extension of his free-association treatment to have me write down my own past. Feeling that I could rely on his duty of professional secrecy, I decided to record the experiences I had until then revealed to no one. At all events, some of these must already have leaked out in the course of the amytal interviews to which my doctor had subjected me, and I felt inclined to let him know the details—not that he could be expected to understand most of what I was saying.

This doctor of mine is a fool. He is five years younger than I. He is constantly sniffing up mucus into his insectivorous nose. He is totally unaware that after my repatriation I did research on the symptoms of schizophrenia and retrograde amnesia and that I came to this institution of my own free will. His knowledge of psychiatry is on approximately the same level as mine of theology.

By applying various tentative methods, such as artificial hibernation and shock treatment, he cured me of my habit of rejecting food, thus subtracting one source of inconvenience from my everyday life; for this at least I am grateful to him.

The money I received from selling my house seems to allow me to bury myself for the time being in this peaceful private room. I refuse to have a nurse in my room, let alone my wife. I offered my wife a divorce and to my surprise she accepted it. A sort of sentimental understanding arose between her and my doctor out of their common interest in my illness, and as I sit here I am well aware that though she has stopped coming to see me, she still visits that forest of red pine trees in front of the hospital to engage in amorous encounters with the doctor.

I don't care. Just as all men are cannibals, all women are whores. Each of us must act according to his nature.

The doctor has read my notes up to the point where my memory breaks off. Chuckling fulsomely, he says: "It's very well written. It reads just like a novel, you know. . . . It's a shame that shock of yours blocked out the last part of your memories," he adds after a while. "We've got a good idea that this is just where we'd find the clue to your illness. . . ."

Assuredly that forgotten period remains within me like a bright streak in the darkness. I try to direct the spotlight of my memory into the past, but as soon as it reaches the moment of the rain-spattered breechblock, it undergoes, so to speak, a total reflection and I can penetrate no further. Yes, perhaps it is in the ten-day period between that moment and when my memory starts again on the operating table of the American field hospital that I may find the link which can join my present existence with my past memories from the Philippine mountains.

In the absence of any memory images from the period, I resolve to enter that unknown territory by means of deliberate reasoning; for reason, too, can be effective in the process of recollection.

Having fixed me with his eyes, in which I can detect the self-satisfied expression of one who believes that he understands another's mental condition, the doctor nods and leaves my room. I go out by myself into the garden. I sit down on a bench and observe how the long shadows of the October sun cover the pines, how they fall onto the yellowish green of the lawn, bringing into relief a host of purple speckles; and my mind, newly stimulated by my conversation with the doctor, starts to spin the thread of reasoning. . . .

It was in the Ormoc area that the guerrillas captured me—or so at least it was stated on my P.O.W. tag. Yet the last place I remember is a mountain forest at some considerable distance from the guerrilla country by the coast. So I must have walked. But with what aim in mind could I have walked?

Since the night following my murder of the Filipino woman, when I had thrown away the weapon I regarded as the cause of my crime, this was the first time that I had deliberately grasped a rifle in my hands. I had kept the rifle even after killing that cannibal Nagamatsu; from this fact I can assume that I continued to carry it during my period of oblivion. Was this not a sign that I was still resolved to represent God's wrath?

But no, there is no such thing as God. His is an existence so tenuous that it depends entirely on people's disposition to believe in it. The question is: was I really under the illusion that I represented divine anger?

The idea of Filipinos was for me entwined with that of prairie fires. Whether they were bonfires to dispose of waste husks, or grass being burnt to encourage the growth of new pasturage, or smoke signals to inform distant comrades of the presence of us Japanese soldiers, there was in my mind, as I roamed about by myself after being separated from my unit, a causal relationship between these fires and the Filipinos whom I imagined crouching beneath them.

Is it possible that I may again have seen a fire in those plains?

Deep in my ears—or is it in the bottom of my heart?— I seem to hear a muffled sound, as of drums beating in rapid succession. Their drawn-out roll falls on the ever-lengthening shadow of the red pines in front of me; it falls on the image of the prairie fires, which in the solitude of the Philippines followed ever ahead of my footsteps.

Now here on the level Musashi Plain that stretches out round the hospital, I feel that countless prairie fires are rising invisibly into the air. I feel that my gray period of oblivion is dotted sporadically with the reflection of prairie fires. There is no concomitant sensation or thought; that reflection alone is a living reality.

I return to my room. I have my supper and go to bed: even now the rapid tattoo of drums continues. Then finally I recall the entire period that has lapsed from my memory. No, not the entire period; but as I write these notes perhaps it will all come back.

A Dead Man's Writings

Maybe this, too, is nothing but illusion. Yet I cannot doubt all my feelings. Recollection is itself a type of experience—and who can say that I am not alive? Even though I can believe no one else, I still have faith in myself. . . .

A great fire rises furiously in the plain and at the base I see its tongues of flame. There is another fire—narrow, tentative, its top curved like a hook; it quivers like the needle of a magnet and I feel that it can change its shape at will.

Strangely enough, the image of these fires brings with it the image of combustibles. I do not know whether it is under the hooked smoke or under the flame-filled fire that I see it, but I can picture burning chaff piled high like an anthill. The fire itself I do not see, only the smoke—the smoke, which coils round like steam at the top of the pile, moving with difficulty from its source and seemingly reluctant to be scattered by the wind, draws itself together into a compact bundle, and rises into the sky, as though it had some destination in mid-air. Then again I see the spot where the plain has been scorched. Like a shadow moving along the bottom of water, the smoke crawls along over the black, newly burned stubble and threads its way low between the roots of the grass, which has escaped the fire and still stands erect.

The prairie fires are shaped like those I saw after leaving my company. Yet on none of the earlier occasions did I approach their base; my present image of combustibles must therefore belong to the period of oblivion.

In my mind the scorched grass and the burning chaff are intimately connected, almost as if they belonged to the same fire. Surely the fact that they adhere so closely to each other in my consciousness proves that they were close also in point of time.

Yes, I must have seen the smoke and thereupon started to walk toward it.

But to what purpose? This I cannot remember. Again my mind becomes a blank sheet. Yet from my deduction that I walked, a new image rises to the surface of my mind.

It is once more the image of myself walking between the hills and the plains with a rifle on my shoulder. My green uniform has faded to a light brown and there are holes in the sleeves and shoulders. The figure is barefoot. Yes, from the indentations of his emaciated neck as he walks a few paces ahead of me, I can tell that this is certainly I, First-Class Private Tamura.

But then who can be this "I" who is now looking at the

figure? It also is I. After all, who is to say that "I" cannot consist of two people?

The surrounding nature is soundless, as if it were under water. These hills and trees and stones and grass all seem to have floated down through the lofty space to settle here at the bottom of nature. High in the heavens God created it all; then He let it sink down to the bottom. He deigned to have it pierce that great body as it descended vertically to its present position.

The surrounding nature is a motionless form which has already used up the time that God granted it for sinking and which now can sink no further.

I, a haughty human driven by somber passions, walk through this eternal space with my rifle resting on my shoulder. My gait is unruffled, as though I were a stranger to such a thing as starvation. Where am I going?

I am on my way to the prairie fires, to the place where the Filipinos live. I am on my way to chastise all those humans as they crawl sideways over the globe that faces God vertically—those humans who give pain to God.

But if I am an angel of God, why am I so grieved? Why is this heart of mine, which should now be free of all earthly attachments, so full of uneasiness and fear? I must make no mistake. . . .

From the hill rises the prairie fire. Swaying like some sea plant, it rises higher, higher, still higher.

Where does the sun dwell? Like God, it, too, must be above that sky, even above the water that fills the space.

The grass on the hilltop bows under the flow of the water. The fire faces the low, black forest that encircles the summit, and it flies as if escaping from some pursuer.

He is there—yes, a human being is there on the hilltop. I fire my rifle. I miss. He runs crouching down the slope, and when he is out of my range he straightens his back with assurance and disappears briskly into a forest.

There are others, also. The tops of their bodies emerge above the swaying grass. One, two, three people . . .

They approach. Now crouching, now bobbing up one after another like robots, they approach me over the swaying grass with their dark, featureless faces. No, I must no longer make any mistakes.

Where is the sun?

Now the fire has come. It approaches quickly—that senseless fire—burning the grass that surrounds me. With its neck raised and its mouth open, the fire draws near. Behind the smoke, the human beings are laughing as ever.

It is nothing serious, nothing serious.

I see myself quietly raising my rifle—my rifle with its crossed-out chrysanthemum crest. What supports it from below is my beautiful left hand, the part of my body of which I am most proud.

At this moment I feel a blow on the back of my head. A numb sensation spreads to the extremities of my body. Yes, of course, I had forgotten—this is when I was hit. So the matter is settled. What I have hoped for ever since the day I entered this hospital is death—and now at last it has come.

But why then do I subsist? Although I cannot see them, I can be seen by them and they can handle me just as they wish. They can lay me on their operating table and reset my fractured skull and do whatever else they please.

I had thought that when people died their consciousness ceased. I was mistaken. Things do not come to an end even with one's death. I must tell this to my fellow men. I call out: "I'm alive!" But my voice does not reach even as far as my own ears.

Albeit that they are voiceless, dead people continue to live. There is no such thing as individual death. Death is a universal event. Even after we die, we are constrained to be permanently awake and day after day to continue making decisions. I should let all mankind know of this; but it is too late. . . .

On the deserted plain the grass continues to sway round about me with that same eternal motion I saw when I was alive. In the dark sky the sun glows still darker, like obsidian. But it is too late. . . .

Through the grass the people approach. They seem to glide forward, sweeping aside the tall grass with their feet. They are the people who now inhabit the same world as I, the people I have killed—the Filipino woman, Yasuda, Nagamatsu.

The dead people are laughing. If this is indeed celestial laughter, how awesome a thing it is!

At this moment a painful joy enters my body from above. Like a long nail, it slowly pierces my skull and reaches to the base of my brain.

Suddenly I understand. I know now why they are laughing. It is because I have not eaten them. I have killed them, to be sure, but I have not eaten them. I killed them because of war, God, chance—forces outside myself; but it was assuredly because of my own will that I did not eat them. This is why in their company I can now gaze at that dark sun in this country of the dead.

Yet perhaps while I was still alive as a fallen angel

armed with a rifle I did really aspire to eat my fellow men as a means of chastisement. Perhaps my secret desire, when I saw those fires in the plain and set out in search of the people who must be beneath them, was precisely to fulfill this aspiration.

If, at the very moment I was about to fall into sin through my pride, I was struck on the back of my head by that unknown assailant . . .

If, because I was beloved of God, He vouchsafed to prepare this blow for me in advance . . .

If he who struck me was that great man who on the crimson hilltop offered me his own flesh to relieve my starvation . . .

If this was a transfiguration of Christ Himself . . .

If He had indeed for my sake alone been sent down to this mountain field in the Philippines . . .

Then glory be to God.

A NOTE ON THE AUTHOR

SHOHEI OOKA (*pronounced "Oh-ka") was born in Tokyo in 1909. He specialized in French at Kyoto University, and was graduated in 1932, after which he made a name as a translator of French literature. In 1944 he joined the Japanese Army, and was taken prisoner in the Philippine defeat of 1945. In 1953–4 he was a Fulbright Visiting Professor at Yale University, and at present lectures on French literature at Meiji University in Tokyo.*

He is the author of a war diary, RECORD OF A POW (1948), and of two novels, THE LADY OF MUSASHINO (1950) and FIRES ON THE PLAIN (1952). He has contributed short stories and critical essays to almost every literary magazine in Japan, and has been awarded two literary prizes: the Yokomitsu Prize in 1949 for his first book, and the Yomiuri Prize in 1952 for this one. He now lives in the beautiful coastal town of Oiso, not far from Tokyo, with his wife and two children.